# A Trumpet in Darkness

# A

# TRUMPET IN DARKNESS

## Robert G. Hughes

SIGLER PRESS
Mifflintown, PA

Copyright   1997  Robert G. Hughes

Reprinted with permission by Author

by

SIGLER PRESS

First Reprint Edition

1997

Library of Congress catalog card number 97-069506

# Contents

# Preface

The twelve-year-old boy felt lost. The opening campfire was over, and he was back at the cabin with seven strangers. Soon everyone was in the sack. Lights were out. From under the covers, in the upper bunk by the front window, the new camper could see the softball field bathed in moonlight. The chirping of the crickets was a sinister sound. The adolescent had never felt so alone in his life. Though parents and friends were less than ten miles from Camp Greenwood, home seemed gone forever. Then he heard it. The sound of a trumpet sent shivers up and down his spine. The words of "Taps" echoed through his brain. "Day is done. Gone the sun, from the lake, from the hills, from the sky. All is well, safely rest. God is nigh." In my first night at camp, a trumpet in darkness was a note of hope.

Years later, as a student at the Lutheran Theological Seminary at Philadelphia, the image of the trumpet took on further meaning. Dr. Martin J. Heinecken, Professor of Systematic Theology, prefaced each syllabus in the introductory dogmatics course with a quote from 1 Cor. 14:8: "If the trumpet-call is not clear, who will prepare for battle?" (NEB). For Dr. Heinecken, one central task of systematic theology is to reflect upon the faith, so that God's Word can be taught and preached plainly. I left the seminary determined that the trumpet of my proclamation would sound distinct and powerful notes.

Yet frustration with my own funeral preaching initially motivated this study. When ordained into the ministry of the Lutheran Church in America in 1962, I was confronted for the first time with the challenge of ministering and preaching to the grief-stricken. I had not served an internship. Even in a classroom setting I had never been forced to struggle with the task of preparing and delivering funeral sermons. Seminary training and limited professional experience had not prepared me to perform this vital function effectively.

I began to read extensively on the subject of death and grief. While this material was helpful, it did cause discomfort. It became evident to me that both my own sermons and the print resources available were theologically and pastorally flawed. They were not in accord with the "theology of the cross" orientation of the seminary. The trauma of loss and grief was muted. Hope, even in my own preaching, seemed restricted to the promise of life after death. Furthermore, these funeral messages did not seem effective in helping mourners to face loss realistically and rebuild their lives.

When I was called to the Lutheran Theological Seminary at Philadelphia, I was determined to give careful consideration to the same area where, as a parish pastor, I had struggled. This book is an attempt to share my findings with parish pastors who face the regular challenge of sounding the trumpet in darkness.

I would like to thank the Board of Directors of the Lutheran Theological Seminary at Philadelphia, who provided the sabbatical leave, and Lutheran Brotherhood, who rendered the scholarship assistance to make this writing possible. Fortress Press has encouraged the study from the beginning. In our team-taught course "Ministry and Death" Professor Leroy Aden and I have developed a unified pastoral and homiletical approach to ministry to the grieving. The Rev. Carl T. Uehling, pastor of St. Matthew Lutheran Church in Moorestown, New Jersey, and an associate in the Academy of Preachers, read the manuscript and offered valuable suggestions. Professor Lyman Lundeen, a faculty colleague, helped to sharpen the discussion in chapter 3. Special appreciation is expressed to my wife, Dona-Lee, and to my family for their support. Let the trumpet sound!

# Introduction

Death is an experience of deep darkness. Survivors are shaken by anxiety almost beyond hope of recovery. This emotional senselessness is compounded by a dread of the future, by turmoil over pressing decisions, and by the need to live again. The thoughts of mourners are a reflection of the chaotic scene about them. Intellectually, there is a need to make sense of what has happened. The world is pitch-black.

A trumpet in darkness is the announcement of the victory of Jesus Christ over death and the grave. The subject of this book will be the proclamation of that gospel to those who have experienced the loss of a loved one through death. Christian preaching that centers in the cross and resurrection of Jesus can enable mourners to face the reality of death and to hope against hope for God's gift of new life.

Funeral preaching is a challenge today. Not so long ago it was common to have a family request that a sermon not be included in the funeral rite. Some Christian traditions relied on the liturgy alone for help and comfort. In this ecumenical age the sequence of lessons, gospel, sermon, creed has found its way into the worship of a variety of church bodies. The recognition that the sermon is integral to a total service, whose effectiveness is diminished without it, commends a return to funeral preaching.

Modern psychology tends to support this decision. There was a time when communication theorists were pessimistic about the ability of mourners to hear funeral sermons. Grief and loss do short-circuit mental processes. Blockages can occur. The attention span is affected. At the same time, mourners may be emotionally ready, open to God's word, in a way that secure individuals are not. With life in chaos, and the need to restore vital balance, defenses are down. It has been the experience of clergy that greater vulnerability leads to heightened receptivity more often than to stubborn defensiveness.

Yet problems remain for the pastor. Many thoughtful individuals feel that old-fashioned eulogies are out of place today. Lay persons are frequently embarrassed by preachers who overstate the goodness of a person's life. They know the deceased far better than the pastor. At the same time, relatives do not appreciate sermons so impersonal that they have a "to whom it may concern" flavor. Further, when the dead person's life and conduct are described accurately, this remembering process is helpful psychologically. So the pastor must somehow tiptoe a narrow line, personalizing the sermon without lauding the dead.

Of course, the mourners are the target of the sermon. In a real sense it is for them. Yet how can sensitive pastors prepare sermons that take into account the location of key mourners on the continuum of grief? If a death has been sudden and tragic, with the anesthetic of shock working its protective magic, one aim of the sermon may be to assist listeners to face death and begin to grieve. Conversely, a protracted death may bring to family members a sigh of relief. Yet such feelings come laced with guilt. How is the pastor to use the sermon, one malleable element within the liturgy, to target the particular feelings and questions of mourners?

The book will deal with these challenges in a straightforward way. In chapter 1, "A Strategy for Communicating with Mourners," the pastor ministers to the family of a woman who has died after a prolonged bout with cancer. As the pastor calls on the family, deals with emotions, and struggles with questions, the contours of the funeral sermon begin to take shape. Chapter 2, "Types of Death," begins with a critical analysis of cancer death, its dynamics, and their impact on the preaching task, before exploring five other types of death. This chapter will be a continuing resource for the preacher. "The Cross in the Face of Death" addresses the various theological questions (spoken and unspoken) that trouble mourners: Why, God?; What did I do to deserve this?; and others. Chapter 4, "The Funeral Sermon," presents a model for shaping these messages that will assist listeners to face the hostile event of death by setting that reality in the context of the gospel hope. The sample sermons at the end of the book are analyzed, so that the reader can see how theory works itself out in practice.

# 1
# A Strategy for Communicating with Mourners

Some years ago, all of my ministry to one of our families came to focus in a private room in the intensive care unit. The room was so small that only one chair could join the night table to break its starkness. Flowers and cards had long ago been removed to make way for pans and instruments.

The patient, Gwen Olson, was about forty-five, and she was dying of cancer. "Her breathing is much worse, pastor," her husband Paul whispered as I came into the room. "Yesterday when you were here she seemed bright, almost hopeful again. Today, I can see her fading before my eyes." A nurse turned from checking Gwen's vital signs. "They run in and out all the time, pastor, but they don't do anything. Doctors. Nurses. Medicines. Nothing helps!"

Outside a siren broke the calm of the quiet neighborhood. Inside Gwen's eyelids fluttered and opened. Her head was tilted to one side. Her eyes looked far away.

"I'm here, Mom." A slim girl, who looked about twenty, moved from one corner of the room to grasp the gray hand. Even as she hurried, Jill was careful not to disturb the plastic tube in her mother's arm.

"Jill," Gwen gasped, "please lift me higher." Gwen was indeed struggling. Her speech was slurred. "Paul, I can't breathe." As Paul and Jill strained, Gwen's head rolled from side to side.

"One, two, three, here we go." Gwen was a few inches higher on the pillow. Paul pressed a button, and the bed edged upward.

"Gwen, it's pastor. Can I pray for you?" There was no response. Eyes were closed again. I moved closer and the family gathered around the bed. The small book was opened.

"Almighty God, look on Gwen, whom you made your child in Baptism, and comfort her with the promise of life with all your saints in your eternal kingdom, the promise made sure by the death and resurrection of your Son, Jesus Christ our Lord. Amen."[1]

Gwen's chest heaved, but her face seemed peaceful. The conscious horrors were almost over.

"Into your hands, O merciful Savior, we commend your servant, Gwen. Acknowledge, we humbly beseech you, a sheep of your own fold, a lamb of your own flock, a sinner of your own redeeming. . . ."[2]

The book was closed, and the wait began. Forty-five minutes passed. An hour. Jill kept walking in and out. Jennifer, her eleven-year-old sister, sat hunched over, guarding her thoughts. Paul stood with his hand over Gwen's. I stepped out to make a telephone call and returned to stand beside Paul. We waited together while Gwen slipped away.

Suddenly a nurse was at the bedside, stethoscope in hand. On the monitor, Gwen's life moved across the screen and flattened. It was over.

If the previous account reads like fiction, that may be because it happens so rarely. In the imaginations of my generation of seminary students deaths frequently occurred with the pastor at the bedside. We pictured the grace of quiet moments around the bed where weeping, talk, and prayer could flow uninterrupted. We saw ourselves standing by to support and comfort in the narrow passage between life and death.

Unfortunately, in ten years of parish ministry I was present only five or six times at the death of a parishioner, and only three times with family gathered in the sort of ideal setting described above. From the point of view of good pastoral care a ministry at the time of death is beneficial. It was prominent in the "When to Call the Pastor" pamphlet I prepared for the congregation and discussed with the church council and adult classes. But the fact remains that it seldom happened. Far more frequently I received a telephone call from the family—if they were active church members. Otherwise the mellow tones of a local funeral director would inform me, "You have a funeral on Wednesday at 2:00 P.M."

## REALITY: TELLING
## THE STORY OF DEATH

In any case, if the mourners are local people, the scene will eventually shift to the home of the family or the dead person. No matter how protracted or limited contact with the family has been, the story of death should be retold there. Sometimes the pastor comes to this encounter with the family from weeks of contact as a loved one lay dying in a hospital or nursing home. Sometimes the pastor is summoned to the home of someone who sat across the table at a committee meeting the night before. No matter—when the pastor arrives for the first visit with mourners, it is important to draw out their painful memories.

Because the funeral sermon is a key public response in a continuing pastoral relationship this conversation following the death of a loved one is one context of preaching. Preachers interpret the biblical text in the preparation of sermons. Exegesis of listeners is equally important. Sharing the story of death is one way for survivors to begin coping with loss. Active listening by the pastor is diagnosis in the service of both pastoral care and preaching.

When death is sudden, without warning, these stories may lack the basic characteristics of story. Time sequence is confused. Events are difficult to follow. Self-expression is halting. Words do not come out, or they do not come out right. Rambling conversation may be evidence of confused mental processes. Shock expresses itself in vacant pauses and comments like, "What can I do?" or "How can I go on?"

At other times stories can be tightly formed. Often when the dead person lingered for a long time, or where death approached in measured strides, there was a need for loved ones to tell the story repeatedly. In the retelling the narrative was shaped and polished.

In the midst of crisis, with frequent interruptions, and little time for a second encounter prior to the funeral, how can the real story of death be determined? How is fact to be separated from fancy? At this moment it is important for the pastor to remember that the task is not first of all to clarify the chronology of death and its immediate aftermath. The mourners' story, the feelings and questions of the grieving family and friends, are the primary concern of the pastor-preacher.

### *Mourners' Emotions*

Mourners will be feeling anxious. Increasingly, psychologists agree that "separation anxiety" (the fear of separation) is an accurate label for the basic feeling of a person who loses a loved one.[3] Anger, depression, and guilt are experienced. Mourners struggle between fantasy and reality.[4] Yet anxiety is the central response to death's loss and is the glue that holds grief's other emotions together.

Unfortunately, people sometimes view the emotional suffering of grief somewhat as they do a cough—an annoying symptom of infection to be restrained or muffled. Well-meaning friends or even family members may discourage mourners from sharing honest feelings with pastor or priest.

Grief is indeed a symptom of death's loss, but beyond that it is a positive weapon in the struggle for wholeness. As the cough gives evidence of infection and helps to clear congested lungs, so grief's emotions are both symptomatic and therapeutic. While they are triggered by death (symptoms in that sense), shared and addressed these emotions can become phases in a journey toward health. By listening actively, the pastor notes emotions as clues for both preaching and pastoral care.

In the case of the Olson family, conversation resumed in the family living room. "She felt as if she was deserting us. She didn't want me to have to raise the girls alone." Paul was speaking. "She was brought up that way. The kids came first. When Jill was a cheerleader we only missed one football game in two years." A tear formed in one eye and ran down. Awkwardly, Paul wiped it away. "I don't know how we'll manage without her."

"You feel alone." The pastor's voice broke the long silence.

"Feel? In some ways I don't feel anything. It's like another world; it can't be happening to me . . . to us. In another way I feel, well . . . relief almost." Paul lapsed into thought again.

Jill rose, almost abruptly, and went upstairs. The pastor noted her silent flight. Jennifer moved next to her dad.

"It has been a tough nine months, pastor. You know she got this cough the week before Christmas. It would never clear up, what with the smoking and all. Jennifer and I, we warned her. When they found it was cancer, in the lung, in the surrounding tissue, they talked to us about an operation. It didn't look good. We hoped the chemotherapy would. . . ." Paul just shrugged his shoulders.

"Mommy never talked about cancer." Jennifer was sitting forward. "Daddy and I talked about it. She was always telling us about how she felt, and the tests. Mommy had trouble saying the word cancer."

"And you, Jennifer?" the pastor probed.

"I really miss her."

"It's over now. That's where I am." Paul was speaking with more force and energy. His hands moved from his lap. "Gwen couldn't get better. That was clear almost from the day Dr. Roberts broke the news. I was angry at first. You know, ten years ago, things weren't going well for us. We almost called it quits. But we put it together. I was really ticked off." Paul's hands sagged. "But all those nights, those endless nights of sitting up with her. You know she couldn't lay flat the last four months. After awhile, I just began to think, well, that it ought to be over." A long pause. More tears. "Jill can't understand that. Pastor, is it wrong to feel relief?"

### Mourners' Questions

Jangled emotion provokes many of the questions mourners ask. Mind and emotions are governed by different kinds of "logic," but they are linked. The mind needs a means to cope with anxiety on the feeling level. The feelings require the level of perception-cognition to make sense of death intellectually. Head and heart assist each other.

In the chaos of death mourners may feel a panicky need for answers. When life becomes so baffling and threatening outside that it appears devoid of order, it is likely that chaos reigns inside as well. Confusion by itself can be tolerated. What becomes intolerable is the threat that the mind cannot make sense of death or life. A frantic need for answers may cause even reasonable individuals to clutch theories that, in retrospect, will appear partial, distorted, or simplistic. In the face of death fear comes out in question marks.

It is important for the pastor to be alert for signs of intellectual bafflement. What are survivors asking? What is the family struggling to understand? Sensitive ministers and priests look for repeated queries. They pay particular attention to remarks that in the course of conversation seem to come from nowhere. The emotional intensity of a statement may betray its urgency. Paul's question, "is it wrong to feel relief?" had this kind of urgency.

Paul had learned in the months of long and irreversible deterioration that sometimes dying is harder to cope with than death. The pressure to act normal, not to break down repeatedly, to bear the brunt of pain and depression finally led him to hope for an end to suffering. Gwen's death came as an answer to prayer.

Because time is short, with a sermon to be prepared in a day or two, the pastor may be more direct than usual. Important but less pertinent issues can be set aside for subsequent visits. Urgent questions are explored immediately.

### The Story Behind the Story

Alongside emotions (how mourners feel) and questions (what mourners ask), the theology mourners hold is crucial for preaching. This theological frame of reference might be called the story behind the story. The story of death (who died and how) is significant. But of supreme importance for proclamation, behind the emotions and questions, is the meaning of that death to survivors.

If the pastor is a sensitive observer and a careful listener, and if mourners are candid, an implicit theology of suffering may begin to take shape in conversation. If it can be discerned, the preacher always begins with the theology people possess. Immature or developed, fledgling or tested, the perspective from which mourners view death is a starting point for preaching.

Frequently this intuitive theology is a far cry from the coherent cross-centered faith of the church. It may be inchoate, comprised of random bits of Sunday-school memories, unrelated images, cultural aphorisms, and personal philosophy. This theology may be discernible in crisis if at no other time.

Paul Olson's feelings had to be reconciled with his theology. The conversation picks up at that point.

"Pastor, is it wrong to feel relief?" Paul looked the pastor straight in the eye. He wanted an answer.

"Paul, feeling relief is perfectly natural under the circumstances. That's what I think. But it's important what you think . . . and feel."

"I'm not sure what I think. I know Jill doesn't understand. She thinks I gave up on Gwen. Sometimes I feel so alone."

"You're not alone, Daddy. I'm here." Jennifer put her head on her father's shoulder.

When death occurs, everything seems up for grabs. Terrifying feelings press to be acknowledged and handled. Questions cry for answers. Decisions must be made. In one sense a mourner is a story in search of an ending. Somehow the emotional suffering of grief and the intellectual confusion of death must be resolved. A sermon remains to be prepared and preached. How will the story end?

## HOPE: RETELLING
## THE STORY OF DEATH

A mourner brings his or her own story, a story of loss and grief, to the first encounter with the pastor. Now it is the pastor's turn. When someone in trouble tells a story, it is both presentation and invitation. A mourner's story cries out for a response. Stories evoke stories.

Retelling the story assists loved ones in shock and pain to face the reality of death. The problem of family members and close friends of the deceased has been called the oyster-shell effect. When danger threatens the oyster buttons its hatch for protection. This instinctive reaction allows him to hide until danger passes, then reopen. Anxious people also button up, but they have trouble reopening. While closure may be necessary to survive the initial onslaught of death, reopening is just as essential. Otherwise a hiding place becomes a prison.

The pastor's retelling of the story may have an altered plot. In part that is because his or her perspective is different. The pastor enters the story of the parishioner imaginatively. While respecting the story told, the minister actually sees the sequence of events and their meaning in another way. So a struggle of stories ensues, with one interpretation contending with another for dominance.

Lest this seem manipulative, remember that the story of death told by mourners is partially interpretation already. Whether the pastor's visit is twenty minutes after death or thirty-six hours later, whether the narrative seeps out in monosyllables or spills over in a torrent of words, what comes from the lips of mourners is (to some degree) an appraisal. Both the apparently objective chronicle (this happened, then that) and the emotionally colored recounting are interpreted story.

In preparation for the retelling the pastor has listened carefully, both for the central core of the narrative and for the mourner's own interpretations. These feelings and attitudes are frequently implicit. Often trial and error, punctuated with gentle probing, are necessary to separate story and interpretation. The minister reflects back to the mourner what was heard as well as what it seems to mean. We pick up the conversation as the pastor begins to interpret what Paul Olson has been saying.

"Paul, you and Jennifer have been through a lot. To watch someone you love suffer, struggle for breath, cry out in pain, that has to tear you apart. When you accepted the fact that Gwen was not getting better, probably couldn't get better, you wanted the suffering over. You told me that you prayed for that. It's OK to feel relief."

"If I could be sure that's all it was. . . ." Paul began with hesitation. "If I were positive I felt it for Gwen."

"You wanted it over for Paul too." It came out more like a statement than a question.

Paul simply nodded. "Sometimes you can't stand another day."

### Label Emotions

Labeling emotions may assist mourners to fathom and acknowledge what they have kept hidden, even from themselves. Often a person senses but cannot express what lurks inside. Labeling the emotion helps the survivor to "see" the terror. No longer nameless, but conceptualized, it can be confronted and explored.

Few people can give a concise definition of fear, guilt, or resentment. Yet most of us use these terms and have a common-sense feel for what each means. If labels can be attached to emotions during the initial visit, the labels will assist mourners to recognize their own stories later in the sermon.

"You wanted it over for Paul too."

Paul simply nodded. "Sometimes you can't stand another day."

"Paul, let's talk about your feelings. It seems to me that in some ways you are taking the weight of Gwen's death upon yourself. Because the point came, for Gwen and for Paul, that you wanted the suffering over, now you're feeling guilty."

Labels are not necessarily accepted. The pastor must be a person with the authority to label. This may not be the case with a stranger, with a new pastor, or with one whose pastoral care skills are suspect. Trust develops slowly. The willingness of the mourner to accept the label might be enhanced if time permitted the gentle exploration of "this feeling" or "that emotion." But because time is a factor, with a sermon to be prepared in a day or two, the pastor is more directive than usual.

"Guilty? I don't know." Paul thought a minute. "I suppose Jill is laying on the guilt a bit." Another pause. "It's the emptiness I feel most of all. Jennifer has been a real strength, but sometimes I feel alone in the dark."

### Focus on Images

Frequently images are used to suggest feelings. The pastor noted that twice Paul had spoken of darkness and isolation. Being alone with ourselves can be terrifying. But instead of saying that directly, Paul spoke about groping along trying to find his way. The literal meaning of darkness is important, but for Paul the more suggestive meaning is primary.

Images are by nature analogical, that is, they bridge gaps from one thought world to another. If a mourner describes death as a storm, an analogy is suggested between loss and the forces of nature out of control. Screaming winds, leaves hurled through the air, and pelting rain suggest chaos inside as well as out. A once calm environment seems angry and life threatening. Images give language to emotions. Images stimulate the imagination.

These functions of images are significant because grieving persons feel more than they reason. Mourners are overwhelmed, confused, anxious. For them, felt thought tends to dominate logical thought. Images that spark imagination and touch emotions can be effective in pastoral care and in preaching.

### Theological Clues

Still, mourners need help with reflection as well as feeling. Another dimension of facing reality and finding hope is sharpening questions and thinking about them. Sometimes, even in an initial conversation, clergy can assist mourners to begin putting life back together intellectually.

The drive to know, the compulsion to make sense of life, caused Paul to blurt out his question. The pastor did his best to help Paul accept the feelings behind the question. But the issue for Paul seemed to be God's view of the matter. "Pastor, is it wrong . . . ?"

The pastor may use a personal image as one way to relate to the mourner's experience. Even if it is not on target the sharing tends to keep the exchange going and may stimulate the mourner to go further. The pastor's goal is to give the suffering person some clue that may be useful immediately as well as later in the funeral sermon.

"Paul, you feel alone in the dark. It isn't pleasant. As a little boy, one of the things I hated most was going into a darkened house by myself. When my father and I would be out somewhere at night he would put the car away around back while I would be sent into the house to turn the lights on. I hated it, but he always insisted, 'There's nothing there to hurt you.'"

"I'm always scared in the dark." Jennifer spoke right up.

"I guess I'm wondering, Paul," the pastor went on, "is there anyone there in the darkness with you?" Pause for a moment. "Is God there?" The question had been sharpened. Paul stared off.

"God must have given up on me when I gave up on Gwen. Sometimes I really feel alone. For months now, maybe twice a week, I have this dream. I'm . . . somewhere, I'm not sure where, way out in the country, beside a deserted road. There are no cars, nobody on foot. It's getting dark, and I'm not sure which way to go. It's frightening . . . and lonely."

Conversations with mourners following death may sometimes yield little or no dialogue. The mourners are in shock, or weeping without control, and a conversation is not possible, at least not at the moment. Neighbors come to "pay their respects" and relatives pop in one after the other. The mortician arrives to make funeral arrangements. The conversation never gets going—or if it does, it goes nowhere. What is the pastor to do? In this situation the pages that follow will be especially helpful. The types of death discussed in chapter 2 give clues to the feelings and questions of mourners. Rather than relying simply on weak hunches left over from dead-end conversations, this chapter will assist the pastor to get a preaching "angle."

The section on "Anonymous Death" may be especially valuable.

Paul Olson and the pastor had an established relationship, but more and more these days pastor and survivors are virtual strangers to each other. Clues are needed to enable busy clergy to make contact with the situation and gain insights needed to preach.

Thank God, fruitful conversations with mourners do occur sometimes. It is in these tension-filled encounters that care begins and the funeral sermon is born. Now and then pastors are amazed to hear snatches of a favorite sermon (long forgotten by the preacher) quoted as a helpful insight. More often a hymn text or verse of Scripture with special meaning will be woven into the fabric of conversation. Significant dreams and anecdotes may be shared. These portions of the mourner's own faith story are more useful in proclamation than the favorite hymns and texts of the deceased. If the mourner's theology can be used, the funeral sermon signifies a relationship. It comes with dialogue built in.

### The Good News

Sometimes, when the pastor does get a glimpse of the theology of mourners, it is too distorted for use. Their emotions can be acknowledged; their questions can be addressed; their images can be employed; but their theology may be counterproductive. If the intuitive credo can be formulated by the pastor as heard, and reflected back to the bereaved for acknowledgment, this is a major step. To a bewildered mourner such a confirmation (insightful in itself) can become the basis of later conversation and proclamation. If a few minutes remain for gentle correction prior to the funeral that must be counted an unexpected blessing. Yet, somehow, even in the midst of darkness, the trumpet of hope must sound.

Mourners wait in darkness for the sound of a trumpet. To be sure, they need to face loss realistically, but in the context of new life in Christ and its attendant hope. As the pastor begins to take the lead in conversation there is a need both to deal with the loss and to balance the tendency for pessimistic distortion with the good news.

Christians find this good news centered in the Christ story. Mourners particularly find their identities in the story of Jesus' death and resurrection. Paul goes to the heart of the matter in his Adam-Christ contrast: "For as in Adam all die, so also in Christ shall all be made alive" (1 Cor. 15:22). In the story of Jesus' last days death is overcome in victory. This account has power for believers who "in Christ" have experienced death and the beginnings of new life. In both conversation and proclamation the cross and resurrection of Jesus give courage and hope to believers who face death's contradictions.

But how is the hope of the gospel shared, first in living room and then in pulpit? In the battle of stories we spoke about earlier the entire story of death may not require changing. The pastor may accept the sequence of events and their interpretation up to a point. The mourner's account may be basically accurate or it may be quite distorted. But rather than attempt a total retelling the preacher can "doctor" the ending.[5] Following a tale of seemingly senseless suffering and death, a tragic ending is natural.

Paul Olson, for example, was saying a number of things. "I feel alone." "I gave up on Gwen, and I feel guilty." "My oldest daughter doesn't understand; sometimes I don't understand." "I'm alone in the dark, because even God has abandoned me."

Much of Paul's story is accurate, both to his feelings and to his situation. But the tragic story of guilt and abandonment needs an alternative ending, one consonant with the gospel of God's forgiveness and presence in suffering. The pastor will not preach to Paul, at least not now. But the trumpet will be raised.

"Paul, Jennifer, we'll need to speak again after the funeral is over. There are some things we've just begun to open up, and I would like to discuss them with you. But before I go, let me say just one more thing. When the darkness closes in and you feel totally isolated, when others don't seem to understand, when God appears to have abandoned you, you are not alone. I know that's hard to accept now; maybe it's impossible. But try to stay open to God. It has been the experience of Christians, and my own experience as a matter of fact, that it is in the darkness that our Lord is revealed. I may say more about that in the sermon the day after tomorrow."

As the conversation with the Olsons shows, funeral preaching is a process of mutual storytelling. The story of death as told by mourners is retold by the preacher in light of the Christ story. That process begins in the parlor and continues in the pulpit.

## NOTES

1. *Occasional Services: A Companion to LUTHERAN BOOK OF WOR-SHIP* (Philadelphia: Board of Publication, Lutheran Church in America, 1962), 103.

2. Ibid., 107.

3. David K. Switzer, *The Dynamics of Grief* (Nashville: Abingdon Press, 1970), 93, 94.

4. Wayne Oates, *Pastoral Care and Counseling in Grief and Separation* (Philadelphia: Fortress Press, 1976), 53.

5. Dr. Richard Gardner and other therapists have also changed negative and pessimistic endings of stories in counseling disturbed children. See Richard A. Gardner, *Therapeutic Communication with Children: The Mutual Storytelling Technique* (New York: Science House, 1971), 27.

# 2
# Types of Death

Death is not a homogeneous experience for survivors. There are various types of death, each with its own challenges for the pastor-preacher. The dynamics of grief and the questions asked differ depending upon whether death is prolonged or sudden. The decisions to be made vary with a cancer death, a suicide, or Sudden Infant Death Syndrome. While this seems obvious enough, funeral directors report that they hear the same sermons over and over again without regard for the situation.

Without being exhaustive, this chapter will assist clergy to understand the common types of death, with a particular focus on the related suffering and intellectual bafflement mourners experience. Some attention to the diverse theological interpretations people give their pain will complete the analysis a preacher should do prior to preparing a sermon. Even when the person to be buried was on the fringes of the fellowship circle, and the relatives who gather are total strangers, the pastor will have more confidence knowing the syndrome of emotions and questions that relate to each type of death.

## PROLONGED DEATH: CANCER

When a person dies of any lingering illness special problems confront the survivors. The protracted nature of the disease exacts a heavy toll. The family and friends of cancer victims face challenges during bereavement that call for a special awareness on the part of the pastor. Studies indicate that survivors experience a more difficult period of grief and adjustment when cancer is the cause of death.[1]

### Dynamics of Chronic Grief

*Anger* is a common survivor reaction to cancer death. Families tend to feel helpless during the onset and progress of the illness. Good food has little effect. Tender loving care does not seem to improve the condition of one who is dying. Husbands and wives particularly do not feel as if they are active partners in the fight against this killer disease. It is all in the hands of the doctors.

Thus, when doctors fail to halt the spread of malignancy, anger at these caregivers is an instinctive reaction. Because doctors sometimes avoid the terminally ill, moving patients to remote rooms and isolating them in other ways, hostility toward physicians is compounded. Angry patients and their families feel abandoned.

The stigma attached to cancer, which may include an irrational fear of "catching" the disease, causes some relatives, friends, and church members to avoid the patient. Pastors may find themselves making excuses to postpone visits to persons with cancer. The visits are difficult. It is hard to know what to say. As a result, when death occurs the angry reaction of deserted spouses may be, "Where were you when we needed you?"

Anger at God is also common. The prolonged nature of cancer deaths makes them a particularly cruel end. If survivors view the illness as sent by God, perhaps as punishment, then anger is an understandable reaction.

*Depression* is a second emotion that family members of cancer patients commonly experience. The progress of this disease may be marked by trips back and forth to the hospital. Spouses and family members who participate in the care may be worn down physically and emotionally. Hospital stays offer little respite, since patients require the regular presence of family members at bedside. Geared up for an illness of brief duration, families who have accepted a loved one's impending death may be surprised (and even distressed) when the two-month prediction of the doctor drags out to six months or even to a year.

The tendency of cancer survivors to withdraw emotionally only complicates depression. Anger felt toward people who failed to support the family readily shifts to guilt for feeling that way. This lethal combination of anger-guilt, internalized as depression, cuts victims off from the support they need.

### Preparing to Preach

Thus there are a number of variable factors that will affect survivors' ability to deal with cancer death. The length of the illness, the support of family and friends, and the capacity to express feelings all affect a mourner's ability to cope.

One further variable is the state of the body at death. The sight of cancer taking its toll (i.e., deterioration, disfigurement, pain) does not go away readily. Nightmares may persist for months. Yet in retelling the dead person's story as part of the funeral sermon positive images and memories can be put in place of decay. Pleasant memories to which family and friends can relate will be especially appreciated in the sermon.

How do the families of cancer victims understand the suffering they have experienced? If they accept the suffering as an alien but expected part of life in a fallen world, then resignation (and even acceptance) may be the overwhelming response to cancer. If suffering is viewed as punishment for sin, with God cast in the role of executioner, then the pastor will face the angry question *why?* in counseling and preaching. Chapter 3 provides specific resources on pages 51–56 for dealing with anger-related questions in funeral sermons.

Some families of cancer victims come to regard suffering as a test of faith sent by God to produce strength. Suffering is seen as a refining process from which victims emerge purified. The deceased has atoned for sin and has been prepared for heaven. Survivors have been cleansed to live again. In fact, for a *few*, this reaction may turn an apparently senseless event into a time of Christian growth. This coping device should not be dislodged by the pastor, certainly not in the funeral sermon. Nor should it be reinforced, if the pastor regards it as a residue of Old Testament religion to be outgrown later. For most people the conviction that all pain comes from God presupposes a powerful God who tortures people, a God difficult to love. In fact, suffering seldom trains people for anything. It normally leaves fear, anger, and especially depression in its wake. Hints for addressing depression-related questions in funeral sermons are found on pages 60–65 in this book.

Passages appropriate for preaching texts include: Matt. 11:28–29, God gives rest to the weary; John 16:22, sorrow now and joy later;

Rom. 5:1–5, suffering produces endurance, character, and hope; Rom. 8:18–25, set free from decay; 2 Cor. 1:3–5, hope in the acceptance of suffering; 2 Cor. 4:7–18, we suffer now but glory is coming; 1 Pet. 1:3–9, the risen Lord is the basis of hope for sufferers; Rev. 2:10, a crown of life for sufferers; Rev. 7:9–17, sufferers gathered around the throne; Rev. 21:4, no more suffering.

## SUDDEN DEATH: ACCIDENT

In contrast to prolonged death with its chronic grief, sudden and unexpected death results in acute grief.

### Dynamics of Acute Grief

*Shock and disbelief* may overwhelm and engulf survivors. Persons react as if struck by a physical blow. Panic is apt to result. "Shock and panic may recur intermittently for as long as two to five days and the person so affected should be monitored both pastorally and medically throughout this period."[2] It is not unusual for spouses and loved ones to ride an emotional roller coaster from bitter weeping to unbelievable calm. One moment people feel crumpled, the next oddly normal. Grief comes in waves of disorientation and confusion. Mixed feelings of exhaustion, numbness, and aggressiveness are normal. Ministering to a bereaved family at the time of a sudden death demands great patience.

If the sudden death was accidental people assume it may have been preventable. Survivors tend to inquire about causes of the accident. An initial reaction seems to be a search for some individual who may have caused or contributed to their loved one's death.

*Anger* at those who are believed responsible is common. The driver of the other car, the careless pilot, or the trigger-happy teen-ager is blamed. It is more manageable to deal with one concrete villain, at least at first, than it is to discuss highway safety, our crowded skies, or the social conditions that breed gang violence. Persons in shock and panic cannot deal with complexities.

Anger at the dead person may be present too, although it is seldom articulated. Survivors weep for themselves more than for the deceased. The fact that the lost person does not return despite the mourner's angry protest will help survivors to come to grips with the reality of loss. The injustice of being forsaken, with little means of support, or to raise children alone, will cause a nonworking spouse to be particularly angry.

Anger at God's injustice should be expected. It will seem to mourners that God has not observed the rules. Accidents cut life short, and a full life is an expected human right. Heart attacks may wipe out the young before the old, the apparently reputable before the obviously corrupt. The perception will be that God is unfair.

*Guilt* will appear when attention switches from the responsibility of others to personal responsibility. "What could I have done to prevent the accident?" "If only I had kept her home this might not have happened." Feelings of having contributed to the death are natural. They will be especially pronounced if a survivor did contribute directly by driving the car or by allowing unsafe conditions to exist at home or work. If attempts to save the victim fail (e.g., artificial respiration), even a heroic person who risked his or her life to save the victim may feel guilty. Guilt feelings need not be logical or realistic, but they will be experienced by survivors.

So-called survivor guilt has little or nothing to do with blame. These feelings of guilt arise for having survived an accident or disaster in which others perished. Survivor guilt is not for complicity in the death; it is guilt at remaining alive. Older persons especially will feel guilty when children or grandchildren die.

Later in the grief process depression is common, but not at first. Death has been too sudden for life to hit bottom so soon. The bleak and empty days lie ahead for the families of those who die suddenly.

### Preparing to Preach

What variable factors will make accidents more difficult for survivors? Is horror a prominent component of the accident due to the presence of survivors at the death scene or mutilation of the body? If so, in retelling the dead person's story in the sermon a positive final image should be constructed for mourners to remember. Pleasant memories of the deceased will tend to overshadow the horror.

Have loved ones been able to experience emotional release, or is anger still bottled up? God is able to hear complaints. Violent lament allows people to get in touch with feelings God already knows and understands.

How do survivors of an accident victim understand their suffering? Is suffering perceived as the will of God? Coupled with this view may be the feeling that it is not right to question God. It is enough to know that God did it. "The Lord gave, and the Lord has taken away; blessed be the name of the Lord!"[3] Ministers and priests will want to determine if mourners are open to another view.

Where anger at God is in evidence, this can be acknowledged publicly as a common reaction to frustration and helplessness. The world is not fair. The bad don't always die before the good. Tragedies cannot be explained fully, and homiletical attempts to do that while defending God will fall flat. It is enough in the sermon to state that the God we know in Christ does not desire human suffering. There is much about life in this world we cannot understand. Later pastoral conversation can dig deeper into the problem of evil, if mourners desire to pursue it. Specific resources for addressing anger-related questions are found on pages 51–56.

Is suffering evidence to some mourners of an irrational and bizarre world where death is the product of blind chance or capricious fate? If so, the accident may be viewed as a test of the mettle of survivors. Be alert for stoics.

Other mourners may view the accident as punishment for the sins of the victim or their own shortcomings. In this view God sends accidents because we deserve them. Thus guilt will be present. If survivors contributed directly to the death or failed at attempts to rescue, that guilt will be deepened.

There may not be time prior to the funeral to sort out subjectively experienced guilt feelings from "real" guilt. It will be important for the pastor to affirm, in conversation and perhaps in the sermon, that we are valued by God despite our sense of worthlessness. We are loved despite our self-loathing. Called into a relationship with God, guilty believers gain both a history and a future. On the cross guilt was forgiven. In a living fellowship with Jesus, Christians set free from the power of guilt can experience a relationship of trust and acceptance. Pages 56–60 provide further suggestions for dealing with guilt-related questions in funeral sermons.

Passages commonly used as preaching texts include: Ps. 103:15–18, life is uncertain, but God is certain; Matt. 25:13, we know neither day nor hour; Luke 13:4-5, sudden death does not indicate God's displeasure; John 11:32-37, Jesus grieves openly for Lazarus; Rom. 8:28-30, in everything God works for good; Rom. 14:7-8, Christians are free to live or die; 1 Cor. 13:12, in life or death we are God's; 1 Thess. 4:13-14 (15-18), grieve in hope.

## UNTIMELY DEATH:
## CHILD AND YOUNG ADULT

Untimely death may take a number of forms, but the dynamics (i.e., the emotional forces operative in each) are similar.

### Dynamics of Untimely Death

*Stillbirth*, or the death of a child shortly after birth, is a particularly difficult experience because it comes at a time when parents or family are at a pitch of expectancy. At the very moment joyous cries of new life are anticipated a child is born without heartbeat or with only a few hours of life ahead. Parents will want to know what was wrong with the baby *if* that can be determined, but prolonged discussions of "nature's way" of caring for malformed children are inopportune at this moment. A baby carried to term has been lost, and the death needs to be accepted and mourned. Parents who desire should be encouraged to give the child a name. Seeing the dead child may also be a way to help grieving parents give the child an identity.

In pastoral contacts *guilt* may be the overriding emotion and focus of conversation. Mothers may mention strenuous activity, working too long, failure to follow doctor's orders, or an inability to give up smoking. Fathers may confess their ambivalence about the pregnancy. Acknowledging these feelings is a first step to dealing with them.

*Sudden Infant Death Syndrome* (SIDS), commonly known as "crib death," is another untimely death that leaves overwhelming feelings behind. When an apparently healthy child in the first year of life dies unexpectedly, and no cause of death can be determined, it is frequently labeled SIDS. Because crib death occurs in sleep, it used to be thought that the child had suffocated. Autopsies rule this out. At present a number of possible causes are being researched, including damage to the infant's respiratory control center before birth.

Parents will fear for the safety of other children in the household. Even when children are older and the fears are irrational a doctor's reassurance may not dispel them.

*Guilt* will lead most fathers and mothers to accuse themselves despite the fact that science has cleared parents of blame. In asking why a crib death would occur in their family parents are apt to seek explanations in their own relationship to God and the church. Remarks about failure to attend worship or to be involved in the life of the congregation may be evidence of intense guilt feelings.

*Anger* is clearly one emotional trigger for mourner questions when untimely death occurs. The frustration of facing an unseen enemy that slays children frequently fills SIDS parents with rage. The inability to focus this bitterness on a specific disease or virus makes it all the more likely that God will be blamed.

*Accident.* When an older child dies of an accident, the grief is acute. With no time to prepare for the loss, shock is overwhelming. Parents may blame each other. The hours or minutes prior to the accident are replayed again and again. Things done or left undone come under microscopic examination. If one parent or the other is determined to find fault with a partner, the acid of anger and guilt can eat holes in marriage or family relationships.

*Terminal illness.* In the case of terminal illness, a lot of theological wrestling goes on prior to the child's death. During months or years of trips back and forth to the hospital pastors will hear parents questioning God's justice. "Why did N. suffer so?" "Why did God allow this to happen?" "Why didn't God hear our prayers for a cure?" Parents are really questioning why a child, young and innocent, has been cut off at the beginning of life. God has broken the rules by allowing a child to die before older parents.

### Preparing to Preach

We have seen that in the case of untimely death, frequently God becomes the enemy. The death of a child seems absurd and out of place in a world ruled by a kind and loving God. What kind of God is it who allows such tragedies to occur? Pastors can identify with mourners in their struggle by helping them to voice their lament, both in living room conversation and sermon. Clergy must be careful *not* to defend God, but rather to portray God as one who hears and understands their anguish.

Pat answers for tragedy do not satisfy. For example, under no circumstances should it be stated that God took the child because God needed or wanted him or her more than the parents. This statement is biblically and theologically absurd and functions only to compound the anger of mourners. Instead ministers and priests can witness quietly but sincerely to a God who is self-giving, whose Son offered his life for the life of all people, who shares human suffering, and who seeks the best in a less than perfect world. References to Baptism, in which God adopts little ones, will be reassuring to families in churches where infant Baptism is practiced.

In ministering to the family and preparing to preach, other siblings should not be ignored. They may not understand death and may experience both guilt and fear. Pages 51–56 provide further resources for dealing with mourners' angry questions.

When a child dies, mourner guilt may well become a focus of the sermons. Parents of stillborn children and victims of crib death suffer from guilt. Parents who gave their sixteen-year-old permission to drive, who told their twelve-year-old he or she could go swimming in the old quarry, or who signed the permission slip of a nine-year-old for the class trip all feel responsible when tragedy occurs.

Sometimes this guilt is complicated because the parental self-image has been crushed. Father did not know best. Mother did not make a wise decision. At least in retrospect that seems clear. Regret at the failure to live up to the image of being a good parent may block the road to forgiveness for persons burdened with a decision that seemed to result in a child's death.

Pastors can help by encouraging parents to grieve. Later, after feelings are vented, parents may be ready to see that they do not have power over life and death, that they are human and fallible, and that chains of events cannot be controlled. Finally, they may be able to hear the good news that they too are children of a loving God who can reform their self-images and can give them an identity as God's forgiven people. Resources for addressing guilt-induced questions are found on pages 56–60.

Passages used to address the situation of premature death include: Isa. 40:11, an image of God's tender care; Mark 10:13–16, Jesus raises little children; Luke 7:11–17, Jesus restores a son to the widow of Nain; John 10:17–27, Jesus is the resurrection and the life; Rom. 6:1–11, death no longer has power over those who died and rose with Christ in Baptism; Rom. 8:31–39, not even death can thwart God's purpose for our lives; 2 Cor. 1:3–5, God's comfort flows to others; Rev. 7:9–17, God wipes away the tears of those who suffer.

## TIMELY DEATH: OLD AGE

Human ambivalence about death emerges most clearly when an older person dies. At the same time as death may be accepted as a release from loneliness and suffering, both older persons and their loved ones may resist it as inappropriate and premature. While theologians may affirm a natural end for those freed from the curse of death by the crucifixion and resurrection of Jesus, the fact remains that rarely is death welcomed wholeheartedly. Rarely are funerals (even those of aged and infirm persons) easy.

### Dynamics of Timely Death

*Acceptance.* Partial losses do precede and prepare for the acceptance of the final loss. Deaths of loved ones are more frequent as years pass. A senior is often left without spouse, bereft of an occupation and its meaning, with few friends, and with children dispersed. Particularly when illness and deterioration have made life less than livable, the older person may come to accept and even welcome death as release.

Sometimes relatives too are accepting. Some go through the stages of grief by anticipation as a loved one suffers loss of hearing, mobility, sight, or memory. Denial, anger, guilt, and depression may accompany the weakening of a sick parent or grandparent. So while eventual death remains a deep loss, relatives do grow to accept death's inevitability.

*Anxiety.* However, various emotions may blend with or block acceptance. General anxiety is a common response to the death of an older person. When a parent dies, especially in old age, children are expected to take the loss in stride. "In general, our society does not encourage either an intensive display of grief or a prolonged period of mourning."[4] Yet the death of a parent is a major loss at any age, and the need to grieve should not be stifled. An assertive older parent may continue to provide emotional stability for an entire family, so that grown children will feel abandoned in the world when Mom or Dad dies. In addition, the death of a parent may suggest to middle-aged children that they are growing older and that their turn to die is coming.

*Guilt.* Death of the aged in institutional settings (nursing homes or hospital geriatric units) may add guilt to the emotional burden of survivors. If the elderly person elects institutional living, and finds life pleasant in apartment complex or life care facility, then guilt is minimal. But if older relatives are unhappy there, and demand to go home or to live with their children, guilt will accompany death for those who fail to accede to those wishes.

In a multigenerational home family members will find life complicated by the presence of an aged or infirm relative. Tensions over quiet hours, diet, meal schedules, and the discipline of children may lead to resentment or open conflict. Commonly elderly persons complain to the pastor about the younger members of the family and vice versa. If a parent or child wished a grandparent away, even subconsciously, guilt will complicate grief when death does come.

*Anger* is common also when sisters or brothers attempting to care for aged parents revert to the sibling rivalries of childhood. All too frequently children begin to vie for parental approval or possessions, accusing each other of neglect or lack of responsibility. When differences in inheritance further complicate the picture, a pastor may be faced with open warfare while trying to plan the funeral.

### Preparing to Preach

While a number of variable factors like age, length of illness, and the quality of the relationship between the dead person and close relatives will affect attitudes, the pastor should not automatically assume that the funeral of an older person will be easy. People will sense an inherent fairness in the death of those who have lived a full life, but a loved one has been lost and grief will run its course.

If acceptance is the overriding reaction to death, then the tone of sermon and service can be one of subdued celebration. When illness and diminished strength bring death as release, the themes of rest and peace can be appropriate theological clues for mourner reflection.

When a spouse has been left behind in old age, then separation and loneliness may exacerbate grief. The tendency of lonely oldsters to withdraw from human contact and to channel grief reactions into physical illness makes the aged especially vulnerable. If the message of God's presence and comfort can be linked to the promised support of pastor and congregation the sermon will be good news indeed.

Finally, while long life is a gift of God, the fact that someone has survived into eighties or nineties does not prove God's eternal salvation of an individual. Printed funeral sermons display a tendency on the part of preachers to deify ancient saints while preaching them into heaven. Further help in dealing with the question, What happens at death—and beyond? is found on pages 66–73.

Passages suitable for the funerals of older persons include: Psalm 23, an old favorite that still speaks; Psalm 90, God's eternity and human transience; Matt. 25:31–40, come inherit the kingdom prepared; Luke 2:25–32, an aged believer departs in peace; John 14:1–6, room in heaven for those who believe in Jesus; Rom. 8:18–25, our hope is grounded in God; 2 Cor. 4:16–18, outer nature wastes away, but inner is renewed; Phil. 1:21–24, Paul belongs to Christ in life or death; Heb. 11:13–15, a better country; Rev. 21:1–7, God wipes away tears and eliminates death.

## SOUGHT-FOR DEATH: SUICIDE

Emotions that accompany most types of death are amplified in the trauma of suicide.

### Dynamics of Suicide

*Guilt* is complicated by the very nature of a sought-for death. Frequently relatives and friends of persons who commit suicide have warnings well in advance. "Fully 80 percent of all completed suicides do in fact speak of their intentions beforehand."[5] Since suicide attempts may outnumber completed suicides by almost ten to one, suicides without warning are rare. If relatives and friends (doctors or clergy) ignore cries for help, or interpret incomplete attempts as mere attention getting, guilt may plague these survivors.

This guilt often takes the form of self-blame. "If only I hadn't quarreled with her." "If only we could have gotten along better." Harsh words prior to death increase guilt. Spouses, because they are so close to the deceased, are particularly hard on themselves. A less-than-satisfactory marriage may be blamed as a direct cause of death. The child who wished a father or mother dead will be devastated by parental suicide.

The observation of John Hewett is worth noting.

> Suicide is an act completed in solitude, and one person is responsible for it—the deceased. . . . No person can single-handedly prevent a suicide unless that person can live without sleep and spend twenty-four hours a day restraining the potential suicide.[6]

Suicide is not primarily the result of outside pressure; it is a decision of the individual.

*Anger.* Self-blame that springs from guilt may quickly take the form of blaming others, of anger. No one can carry the entire weight of guilt alone. Self-blame is transformed into blaming others as a way to distribute the load.

Anger at the deceased is both natural and justified, yet that does not make it easier to confront or express. Suicide may have been an ultimate weapon. Once struck, the blow at relatives or friends cannot be returned by them. Even if the person committing suicide was seeking escape rather than retribution, spouses and family normally feel deserted. "Survivors feel rage toward the deceased for publicly rejecting them."[7]

Directing anger at others is a way for mourners to avoid blaming the dead person or themselves. Blaming close friends and relatives of the deceased is common. Anyone who may have failed to help or support the suicide victim along the way (including clergy or God) can be a target. The deep need to know who failed and why easily leads to scapegoating. Assigning blame can drive families apart at the very moment they need each other most.

*Shame.* The social stigma of a suicide in the family leaves survivors with feelings of shame. While guilt is rooted in disapproval coming from inside an individual, shame results when disapproval comes (or is suspected of coming) from outside. Shame is a feeling of having done something improper or disgraceful in full public view. This embarrassment is accompanied by fears of losing a good reputation and fears of social isolation.

Although some early Christians impatient for the joys of heaven sought martyrdom, both Augustine and Thomas Aquinas labeled these sought-for deaths mortal sins and forms of murder. The stigma against suicide has a long history. Burial in consecrated ground was denied by the church. Legal taboos included relinquishing all of the deceased's property to the state. Families of persons who committed suicide were stigmatized by their communities.

The shift to viewing suicide more as a sickness than as a crime has eased but has not eliminated public censure and shame. Gossip abounds. Friends don't know what to say to survivors. It is normal, even if regrettable, that people scrutinize the life and relationships of the suicide victim to determine who and what contributed to the death. Sometimes tactless remarks by acquaintances cut mourners deeply.

Thus the effect of shame is intense isolation. Survivors and their friends pull away from each other. Especially when mourners are attempting to keep the cause of death secret, and when they are not sure how much others know, communication is adversely affected. There seems to be no one with whom to share the secret or talk through the feelings.

Therefore it is important for the bereaved to accept the death as suicide and to be open about that with others. Attempting to live with a terrible secret that others are likely to know already (or suspect) impedes grief work.

However, pastors may come under great pressure to participate in a denial of the real cause of death as a way to avoid the stigma of suicide. However repugnant this cover-up may be to clergy, the feelings of the family should be respected. It is irresponsible for a pastor to acknowledge publicly something the family of a suicide is not yet prepared to face.

### Preparing to Preach

*If* the family has been able to confront the reality of suicide, and *if* relatives and friends have consented to be open about the cause of death, then the issue should be met head-on in the sermon. Phrases like "took her own life," "killed himself," and "committed suicide" are more accurate than the standard language of death. In public proclamation the term "suicide" will sting like a slap, but once delivered the blow may break through silence and encourage dialogue.

Preachers can assist mourners by becoming the voice of their anger. Cries of desertion can be echoed in the sermon. Obviously, this must be done carefully, so as not to further inflame and interfere with communication. But since feelings of rage are universally felt by survivors, the shock effect of hearing them is mingled with relief that they have been expressed.

The funeral sermon is not the time to attempt to answer all the questions of survivors. Bewildered families cry out, *why*. Yet an examination of motivations cannot penetrate the level of conscious evidence. The one person who may be able to answer *why* is gone. Now only God knows the motives for suicide. It may help if this is stated directly in the sermon.

If the sermon is not a vehicle for addressing all survivor questions it is certainly not meant to rationalize and apologize for the individual who committed suicide. The preacher can evoke sympathy for the victim and understanding in listeners by the way the person's inner and outer struggles are portrayed. At times a bit of this may be in order. But beware; apologies can be just another form of denial.

Wherever possible the preacher should include himself or herself in any guilt that is admitted. Feelings of inadequacy are common to all who touch the life of a suicide. Honestly admitting feelings of self-blame may be one way the preacher can free mourners to accept their own guilt feelings.

Of course, clergy must come to grips with both their personal feelings and their church's teaching about suicide. Acknowledgment of sin as a universal human condition is an appropriate background for dealing with willful actions. To be sure, the destruction of life is a serious abuse of God's gift of life and freedom, yet the believer who commits suicide is in the arms of a merciful God.

Therefore the message of the death and resurrection of Jesus Christ is good news for both the victim and the survivors of a suicide. New life is possible beyond anger, guilt, and shame.

Passages suggested for preaching at the funeral of a suicide include: Psalm 139, God knows the struggles of the living; Matt. 7:1-5, it is God's prerogative to judge; John 3:16, whoever believes in Jesus shall not perish; John 5:24, those who hear and believe pass from death to life; John 10:27-28, Jesus' sheep are safe; John 11:21-27, the risen Lord is the source of life; John 14:25-27, the Holy Spirit imparts Christ's gift of peace; Rom. 6:23, the gift of God is eternal life; Rom. 8:1-4, no condemnation for those in Jesus; 1 Thess. 4:13-18, God cares for the deceased.

## AN UNBELIEVER'S DEATH

Should a Christian minister or priest be involved in the burial of an unbeliever? This pejorative term is the one used in much of the literature, so it is important for clergy to come to grips with its implications for themselves and their churches.

Some clergy feel that any being created in God's image is entitled to a "decent burial." While other clergy will concur about the need to treat deceased persons respectfully, they will not feel compelled by reason of call or conviction to officiate at such services. Yet if close family members are Christians, and particularly if spouse or children are members of one's own congregation, a pastor may view the funeral as an essential ministry to perform. If the deceased was an inquirer who died still searching for a belief system, the pastor's decision may be still easier. If the dead person was baptized as a child or adult there may be further incentive for some. While a person's absence from worship, lapsed membership, chronic unchurched status, or life style may call a living faith into question, a strong conviction about the efficacy of Baptism coupled with the doctrine of the hiddenness of the church may lead a pastor to accede to the family's wishes. Every minister knows unchurched persons, offended at the institution or "sitting out a pastorate," who give other indications of being believers.

### Dynamics of an Unbeliever's Death

It is important to note that, strictly speaking, this is not a type of death. The category indicates the belief system (or lack of one) of the deceased rather than the way in which death occurs. Therefore, in order to determine the full reaction of survivors, it will be necessary to reexamine on the preceding pages the dynamics associated with the appropriate type of death (e.g., sudden, timely, etc.). At the same time, it is clear that the death of someone whose relationship to Christ and the church is questionable does present particular challenges for clergy.

*Guilt* is a common survivor reaction to the death of an unbeliever. "How could I have helped N. to believe?" "If only I had done more to share my faith!" Family members may blame themselves for the fact that a spouse, parent, or child did not seem to trust in Jesus Christ. For some Christians, normal feelings of despair are deepened because death seems to erase any hope that loved ones will be saved.

*Bargaining* behavior on the part of survivors is common when an unchurched loved one dies. In the confused mental processes of mourners, a church funeral or a large contribution may seem ways to make an impression on God. The social need for public approval may result in pressure on the pastor to make the sermon falsely positive and affirming.

*Anxiety* about not seeing a dead spouse or child again may raise the question, Where is N.? Rarely is the query put more directly, Is N. in hell? No matter how the question is phrased, it will be important, initially, to determine what lies behind it. Is guilt speaking? Is the question raised seeking the pastor's reinforcement for the mourner's felt no? Or is the inquiry honest and pressing?

### Preparing to Preach

Variable factors already mentioned will ease or complicate sermon preparation. Is the so-called unbeliever an atheist, an agnostic, a

member of a non-Christian religion, a seeker, or an offended but baptized Christian? Each will be viewed a bit differently by pastor and
people. Other variable factors related to the length of illness and type
of death should not be forgotten. A particularly prolonged, premature, or horrible death may be taken as evidence of God's retribution.

If family members view God as executioner, with death the punishment for unbelief, anger at God may complicate the grief process.
Though passages may be cited to the contrary, the overwhelming
weight of New Testament evidence is that unbelief does not affect
either length of days or type of death. Whatever judgment may be
reserved for those who deny God's offer of grace culminates following
the biological end.

In respect to what he called "problem funerals" Andrew Black-
wood advised pastors to say nothing specific about the deceased when
there is nothing specific to be said. In respect to the ultimate "fate"
of the dead person that axiom remains sound. Pastors are not to
preach the dead into heaven or hell. As W. A. Poovey reminds us, "the
preacher is not the judge of the dead and he is not called on to wound
the living."[8]

Frankly, in my parish ministry I never turned down a funeral
because the deceased or relatives were (in some sense) "unbelievers." I
was called to proclaim the gospel of God's forgiving love in Jesus
Christ, and I did that at every opportunity. Who needs the gospel more
than those who seldom hear it? Normally, these liturgies were con-
ducted in funeral establishments, not in the church building. I did not
preach the dead into heaven or hell; I left him or her to God. To my
way of thinking, the fine relationships with Christ established or rees-
tablished when the posture of the church is seen as open and inclusive
validate a ministry to all persons during the crisis of death.

However, clergy who use funerals aggressively to evangelize unbelievers lack both pastoral sensitivity and common sense. For every person frightened into some kind of affirmation of faith there are two or
three others turned off by the boorish behavior of the preacher.

Whatever comfort can be proclaimed honestly is in order. In telling
the story of the dead person preachers can affirm an individual's place
in the lives of survivors. The joys and benefits of those relationships can
be pointed to honestly. Yet comfort based on the hopeful assurances of
Scripture for believers is inappropriate. It is sufficient to leave the

deceased to God and to direct the sermon to the needs of mourners. Pages 66–73 will give further assistance with the question, What happens at death—and beyond? However, these issues are better handled in pastoral care and in regular Sunday preaching.

It is difficult to find suitable biblical texts for preaching at the funerals of inactive or lapsed members, since by its very nature much of Scripture is communication addressed to the committed. Some pastors seek passages in the early chapters of Genesis or elsewhere that affirm God's care for the whole creation. Psalm 90 is a reminder of our transience and God's endurance. Psalm 139 affirms that God knows us thoroughly. For those who turn to God at the last, the prayer of the thief on the cross (Luke 23:43) may be appropriate. A few clergy find help in John 10:7–16, where Jesus is shepherd of all the sheep. Others look to Romans 9—11, where Paul wrestles with the question of the salvation of the Jews. Passages like Rom. 10:5–13, a confession of faith in Jesus saves, and Rom. 11:33–36, the wonder of God's providence, are helpful. In the end it may be best to use texts familiar to almost everyone in the culture, like John 3:16, to proclaim God's love for all.

### ANONYMOUS DEATH

Obviously, this is not a type of death in the sense of prolonged death or untimely death. This category identifies the all-too-common situation where either the deceased or close relatives or both are unknown to the pastor.

Should clergy officiate in situations where the first look at the deceased is when he or she is in a coffin? Like it or not, every pastor faces this situation regularly in the early months of a parish assignment. Newly ordained persons, right out of seminary, dread the jarring ring of the telephone in the middle of the night that calls them to minister to nameless parishioners. Even experienced clergy beginning third or fourth calls feel uneasy when summoned to the bedsides or living rooms of strangers. Thank God for church secretaries and lay leaders who know congregational members and can brief their uncertain pastors. Particularly in small towns and rural areas, funeral directors may be a trustworthy source of pertinent information.

Even after years of service in a congregation an awkward situation is created for the pastor when the body of a lifelong member is returned from some distant location for burial. Relatives who live locally may be a source of information. Sometimes old friends or neighbors can be found who will be willing to share the story of the deceased. But the real gap may occur when no relationship exists between the minister and the mourners who will attend the funeral. It is difficult for a pastor to express solidarity with suffering persons who are essentially strangers.

Many clergy refuse to conduct the funerals of persons who are not or who have never been members of the congregations they serve. These pastors wish to avoid the dissatisfaction that attends the anonymous funeral. Further, they may be reacting to fellow clergy who are known as "hearse-chasers." On the other hand, these anonymous decedents may well be active Christians. Their own pastors may be ill, on vacation, or unavailable. Frequently local pastors "cover" for each other as a matter of convenience and professional courtesy. Most of these share the deeper motivation of desiring by their actions to testify to the unity of the one, holy, catholic, and apostolic church of Jesus Christ. When requests come from funeral directors who are friends, or from their own members who are relatives of the deceased, it is difficult to say no.

### Dynamics of an Anonymous Death

When called to officiate at the funeral of an anonymous believer, or when those persons attending are not known to the pastor, the dynamics are the great imponderable. Has the dam of emotion broken? Observation may yield clues, although social pressures also bring tears to the eyes of mourners. Are survivors feeling angry or guilty? Veteran pastors, no matter what their normal practice may be, attend the viewings of anonymous persons. Conversations with relatives and friends do yield biographical data and may provide clues to the feelings and questions of those who will attend the funeral.

Even in cases where there is no viewing, where attendance by the pastor is impossible, or where the mourners and the corpse arrive just prior to the service, knowledge of the type of death will give the preacher clues to the inner turmoil of worshipers. A glance at the appropriate section of this chapter will be a reminder of the feelings and questions that are apt to lie just beneath the surface.

## Preparing to Preach

Where funeral preaching is regarded as one party simply telling and the other party simply listening not much communication occurs. Particularly in this kind of impersonal situation, if the ordained person regards preaching as his or her task alone, with mourners the passive consumers of the product, real barriers to communication may be erected. Mourners will tend to withdraw into their own thoughts and feelings and "wait out" the anonymous preacher up front. This would be unfortunate.

Generally, mourners desire to be active partners in the communication process. If pastors really expect preaching to be dialogical, "address and response between persons in which there is a flow of meaning between them," then there is the possibility for a real encounter.[9] J. Randall Nichols reminds us that "one of the best-kept secrets of homiletics is that people are trying to make connections between what the preacher says and where they live."[10] This is true even when preacher and congregation do not know each other, or do not know each other well.

Unfortunately, when preachers face people they do not know they tend to revert to a heavily content-oriented approach. The first instinct is to pull out of the files a "general" sermon on death and to preach it. This didactic style relies on telling it like it is, or like the preacher thinks it is. Books of funeral sermons are full of examples that sound more like theological lectures than sermons. True sermons are never "general." By definition they address the gospel to listeners wrestling with a specific death, disturbed by particular feelings and questions.

The sermon design to be sketched in chapter 4 takes the feelings, questions, and experiences of listeners seriously. But in a situation where preacher and people know each other only on the surface some adaptations must be made.

Pastors use imagination in finding a point of contact with the situation of the deceased person. A visit to the residence can yield valuable information. Is there a piano in the house? What sheets of music are worn from use? If there is a hymnal on the piano, are favorites marked? Is there a Bible on display, and are favorite passages indicated? If family pictures are in evidence, how are these displayed? Does the arrangement of furniture suggest the life style and personality of the person?

Neighbors often know the deceased far better than relatives. Talk to people next door. Who were the person's best friends in the neighborhood? What hobbies did she have? What organizations did he attend? Did she appreciate humor? Did sports trivia fill his conversation? What did this person like to read?

Telephone calls to relatives in distant places may be a source of information. Where was the person born? What does the birthplace suggest about roots? In what year was the person born? Were there famous persons born that year whose lives affected this life? Is the date significant in history? Did life begin in the midst of good times, depression, or war? What was the educational background of the deceased? Where was she employed? Was he a military veteran? With just a little effort it is amazing how much can be discovered.

However, under no circumstances should a preacher pretend to know the dead person when this is not the case. When memories of the deceased are shared in the sermon these should not be related as firsthand information. Phoniness is resented. Credibility suffers. A preacher could say, "I wish I might have known N. twenty years ago when he lived in this community" or "I have been told that N. was an active member of St. John's until she moved away." Do not bluff.

Preachers who are able to share their own struggles and faith in an honest way may be able to draw strangers into the sharing. As we have said, stories beget stories. You tell one and others will too. Mourners who hear the pastor's ideas, feelings, and experiences may be drawn from the sidelines into dialogical conversation.

What can the preacher share? We have indicated that knowing something about the onset and progress of the illness and about the type of death will give preachers important clues as to the feelings and questions of mourners. In addition, what the preacher has felt or experienced personally in the face of this type of death may enable him or her to get a preaching angle. Carl Rogers is credited with the insight, "What is most personal is most general."[11] In other words, what each one of us experiences uniquely and personally others are apt to be experiencing as well.

It is my conviction that the preaching texts most effective in anonymous situations are those known and utilized most widely. These always seem appropriate: Psalm 23, the shepherd leads through dark places; John 3:16, the gospel in miniature; John 11:25, Jesus is the source of life; John 14, room for all; Rom. 8:31–39, not even death separates believers from God.

It is important for the preacher to recall that the funeral is not simply for the immediate family and close friends. A funeral is for the worship of God on the occasion of the death of a believer. All who attend comprise the congregation, no matter how close to the deceased they may have been. All will be wrestling with the great realities of life and death. If the narrow circle of listeners, the congregation within the congregation, is unknown, there is still this broader circle to be addressed with the good news.

This final note is most important. The good news of the death and resurrection of Jesus is the basis of all Christian communication. The pastor is called to officiate because of his or her commitment to Christ as Lord. The gospel assures that Jesus died for the preacher, he died for N., and he died for anonymous mourners as well. The reality of the Redeemer's pain and suffering will connect with the experience of all sufferers who believe. The hope of new life that Jesus gives is not dependent on personal acquaintance or friendship. Speaker and listeners are one in the Spirit, one in Baptism, one in the Lord. It is this oneness that, even in the darkness of death, permits the trumpet to yield a certain sound.

## NOTES

1. Seymour Shubin, "Cancer Widows: A Special Challenge," *Nursing 78* (April 1978): 56–60.

2. Wayne Oates, *Pastoral Care and Counseling in Grief and Separation* (Philadelphia: Fortress Press, 1976), 38. Oates is particularly helpful in distinguishing chronic from acute grief, 36–50.

3. These words from Job 1:21b appear in various translations in a variety of funeral liturgies.

4. Robert Kastenbaum, "Death and Development Through the Lifespan," in Herman Feifel, *New Meanings of Death* (New York: McGraw-Hill, 1977), 36.

5. John H. Hewett, *After Suicide* (Philadelphia: Westminster Press, 1980), 23. Pp. 15–31 are especially useful in puncturing myths and establishing facts about suicide.

6. Ibid., 75, 76.

7. Ibid., 48.

8. W. A. Poovey, *Planning a Christian Funeral: A Minister's Guide* (Minneapolis: Augsburg Pub. House, 1978), 38.

9. Reuel L. Howe, *The Miracle of Dialogue* (New York: Seabury Press, 1963), 37.

10. J. Randall Nichols, *Building the Word: The Dynamics of Communication and Preaching* (San Francisco: Harper & Row, 1980), 45.

11. Cited in Donald Capps, *Pastoral Counseling and Preaching: A Quest for an Integrated Ministry* (Philadelphia: Westminster Press, 1980), 27.

# 3
# The Cross in
# the Face of Death

The theology of the cross provides a resource for clergy in responding pastorally and homiletically to the questions of mourners, because it faces the despair of death even as it proclaims the hope of the gospel. What is this theology?

## THE THEOLOGY OF THE CROSS

The saving significance of the death of Jesus is the focal point of the theology of the cross. The Christ who felt abandoned by God brings God to those who also feel abandoned. The Christ who suffered brings salvation to sufferers. The Christ who died and rose again brings new life to the dead and mourners. The theology of the cross affirms that the cross of the risen Christ is the key to overcoming suffering.

The cross was at the center of St. Paul's understanding of the gospel. In the Letter to the Romans, righteousness through faith in Christ was the formulation he stressed. But in the Corinthian correspondence, Paul accented the cross. He did so to proclaim a God of grace rather than the God of sheer power that the world automatically expects.

To a congregation who believed that the cross was forgotten at Easter's dawn, the apostle taught that the form in which we have the exalted Christ is the crucified Christ. To a congregation who believed that suffering was over for Christians, Paul wrote that Jesus' victory over sin and death is visible only to eyes of faith. To believers exchanging the cross for glory, Paul recalled his own preaching: "For I decided to know nothing among you except Jesus Christ and him crucified" (1 Cor. 2:2).

Centuries later, at Heidelberg in the spring of 1518, Martin Luther placed his theological paradoxes in explicit opposition to the prevailing theology of the church of his day. The reformer used the formula *Theologia crucis* (theology of the cross) because it focused the distinctiveness of the gospel over against the prevalent theology, which he called a theology of glory. Here too the cross meant trust in God's suffering love; glory suggested clear-cut answers like "works" and "merit."

It is necessary to ask in what way the dogmatic position of Paul and Luther is relevant for individuals facing grief and loss in the twentieth century. Douglas Hall is correct when he says:

> The search for a theology of the cross is simply a search for what is fundamental to Christian belief. Perhaps it is even misleading to call it by this special nomenclature.[1]

Yet by employing the label "theology of the cross" the fact is underscored that it is not the only way of expressing Christian theology. However, it is the conviction of this author that cross-centered theology is a perspective particularly fitted to address the gospel to mourners.

The theology of the cross affirms that God is unconditional love. Because God is love, divine sensitivity to suffering is at God's very heart. While it is true that God is powerful, for the sake of human freedom God has renounced complete control of earthly events. Therefore, some things that happen in the world are counter to God's will of love. God suffers when people suffer, because God shares everything with them. God agonizes when people die prematurely or are eaten away by disease, because God allots to each a full life span. God mourns when human beings lose those dear to them, because God knows their pain. The theology of the cross acknowledges that suffering is part of the essence of God, that it is God's genuine power. God is able to take on all the suffering of the world—without being destroyed by it or deviating from God's purpose of love.

Mourners who live beneath the cross of Jesus experience ambiguity. Because they seek to love as he loved, the followers of Jesus are vulnerable to grief-related suffering. Because they feel forsaken, God may seem far away when they need support most. Because they see dimly, answers to the questions suffering raises are always partial and tentative.

Yet Christians know that God has chosen suffering and death as a vehicle of redemption. Christians experience the divine presence in the midst of pain and need. Christians often acknowledge in retrospect that God was able to use suffering to define personality, to give depth to character, and to bring people to salvation.

In short, the theology of the cross takes sin and death seriously. It affirms the truth that humans are in need of salvation and new life, and that they cannot achieve these for themselves. Therefore cross-centered theology focuses on the grace of God and the hope that only God can provide. Hall calls it "a thin tradition which tried to proclaim the possibility of hope without shutting its eyes to the data of despair."[2]

Luther's statement *Crux probat omnia* (the cross is the test of everything) draws the further implication that the Christ of Golgotha is the inner criterion of truth, the test of whatever calls itself Christian. Thus a shorthand definition can be constructed. A theology of the cross is one whose content centers in the crucified and risen Lord, which in turn becomes a perspective from which Christian theology and practice are guided and measured.

At the same time as this theology is constructive, having the potential to give form and meaning to the experience of sufferers, the theology of the cross is polemical. This tradition seeks to come to terms with current views that (from its perspective) seem to compromise the gospel. In the face of death the polemical side of a *Theologia crucis* champions revelation against speculation, faith versus sight, struggle in opposition to achievement, the cross against glory. The theology of the cross can assist mourners to face the reality of death even as it sounds the trumpet of hope.

## A PROCESS OF CORRELATION

The reader may be surprised to discover that each theological question addressed in this chapter is rooted in a brief discussion of one emotion associated with the grief process. Undeniably, the mind and the emotions are related. In doing research for this book I was struck by the correlation of particular dynamics of grief and specific theological questions. People I identified as angry tended to ask the question, *why*, of God. Mourners experiencing guilt feelings frequently inquired what they had done to deserve the death of a loved one. For a time I wondered whether the emotions triggered the questions, or conversely, if theological dilemmas invariably came emotionally valenced. The only thing that can be stated with any certainty is that particular questions, attitudes, and emotions occur together.

In medicine and in other fields a syndrome is a group of symptoms that together are characteristic of a specific condition. Syndromes are clustered symptoms of a problem. Thus this chapter links brief discussions of anger, guilt, depression, and anxiety to theological questions that seem to attend them. Because the pastor-preacher will frequently find them linked in a ministry to mourners it seemed best to deal with questions and related feelings together.

Of course, each section culminates in constructive suggestions for funeral messages. These recommendations are based on the author's content analysis of virtually every funeral sermon printed between 1940 and 1980 and on his own decade of experience in a parish where more than twenty-five funerals a year was normal. However, since no generalizations are consistently accurate guides for individual cases, they should never by applied in a wooden fashion.

### Why, God?

Because ambivalence (love-hate) is a part of every intimate relationship, anger is a predictable dynamic of grief. This hostility may be directed overtly toward the deceased. Normally the grieving person redirects it inward upon the self or outward toward relatives, a doctor, a pastor, or God. To deal with anger, the mourner must be helped to recognize it and confront it honestly. This renders the emotion less potent. However, anger is difficult both to recognize and confront.

Frequently the pastor finds anger masked by other emotions. Mourners are willing to talk about being hurt, frustrated, disappointed, or upset. They may even admit to being annoyed or irritated. But generally they will resist acknowledging hostility or anger. Anger is denied because it is so often regarded as socially unacceptable, an emotion to be repressed rather than expressed, with sanctions for offenders. Mourners will feel guilty about their anger; they may even fear it.

Anger at the deceased for leaving them alone is a common emotion mourners experience. In the case of suicide this feeling of abandonment is easier to understand. The intentional action of taking one's own life leads loved ones to accuse the dead person of desertion. Yet even relatives and friends of accident victims and cancer patients will feel some anger. When a relationship is shaky or somewhat strained, feelings of anger will increase. It is not unusual to hear a wife protest, "He went away and left me to face this alone. How could he do this to me?"

Frequently mourners blame themselves. The simplest instances of neglect or even imagined slights can lead to self-reproach. This self-directed anger, experienced as guilt, will be dealt with more fully later in this chapter.

Caregivers are frequently the targets of survivor anger. The fact that this anger is exaggerated or unreasonable makes recognizing and confronting it all the more difficult. A mourner may say, "I know it doesn't make sense to be angry at Dr. _____. He did all he could." At the same time, anger is what the mourner feels, because the omnipotent healer failed. Or a widow may erupt at the pastor, "I know I have no right to be angry at you. But you preached to me about a God of love, and look what your God did to my husband." It is easier to be angry at God's agent than it is to challenge God.

Hostility directed against God is common, even among committed Christians. A pastor does not spend many afternoons beside hospital beds or in the living rooms of the bereaved before being confronted with the question, *why*. Why did this happen to me? Why has our family experienced a tragic death? Why, God?

In the case of death, *why* is sometimes an instinctive reaction to the loss of a dear one. The question appears and disappears with floods of anger and despair that periodically overwhelm mourners. The question is a symptom of one phase of grief and functions primarily as a safety valve for relieving emotional pressure.

For some mourners, however, *why* expresses a deep wrestling with the question of suffering. It articulates anger, but more than that. *Why* probes at the goodness and justice of God. For some, the reasonableness of the universe is at stake. Pain appears senseless; the world seems absurd in the face of death.

Frequently the emotional lament *why* permeates the intellectual interrogative *why*. C. S. Lewis reports a particularly angry journal notation, in which he accused God of his wife's death. By the next day, the spastic charge had settled into a reasoned question.

Time after time, when He seemed most gracious He was really preparing the next torture. I wrote that last night. It was a yell rather than a
thought. Let me try it over again. Is it rational to believe in a bad God?
Anyway, in a God so bad as all that? The Cosmic Sadist, the spiteful
imbecile?[3]

The emotional and intellectual often fuse in the heat of grief.

What answers the *why* addressed to God? Unfortunately, God does
not provide a rational explanation to the problem of suffering and evil
in the world. There is no satisfactory reason for a child shot to death by
a playmate, for a teen-ager killed by a drunk driver, for a housewife
raped and murdered, for an older person frozen in an unheated home.
Even the Scriptures do not suggest comprehensive and cogent answers
to human pain. Consult the Book of Job.

Or consult Paul. In opposition to the Corinthian theology, which
insisted that knowledge is already perfectly present for believers, Paul
stressed that knowledge is still "imperfect" (1 Cor. 13:1-2). In the age
to come believers will know God with a completeness that now is characteristic only of God's knowledge of them. In the face of suffering
Paul stressed that God's action is concealed and misunderstood in a
fallen world. Only through eyes of faith do believers really see, and
even the sight that faith gives is partial (1 Cor. 13:12). Thus hopeful
believers must be willing to recognize and live with ambiguity until
that day when faith is changed to sight.

What then can be seen? In the Heidelberg Disputation Luther
asserted, "He deserves to be called a theologian . . . who comprehends
the visible and manifest things of God seen through suffering and the
cross."[4] The reformer's conviction was that theologians waste time
puzzling over God's inscrutable will, when in the cross-death God
showed us a heart of love.

The crucifixion of Jesus of Nazareth reveals a God who became a
human being, who becomes one with people who suffer, who is willing
to suffer also. The gospel declares God with us—Emmanuel. God
stands by us in suffering. God supports us in trouble. The cross and
resurrection of Jesus are testimony to God's deep and unwavering love
for us. This good news is the trumpet in darkness.

A more philosophical response to the question *why* is to stress that
God wants the best for us. "Best" should be understood in the sense of
the best outcome in each situation, recognizing that in a world where

evil still exists the best may be only partially good or satisfying. The Old Testament particularly emphasizes that premature and tragic deaths are contrary to God's will.[5] The biblical witnesses agree that God wants a life marked by wholeness, peace, an intensity of satisfaction.

Yet because God has structured the world in such a way that evolutionary process, cause and effect relations, and chance are realities, not all that happens is good or pleasing to God. This is so, especially, because the world is in some sense fallen, less than the perfection God envisioned.

Further, God has chosen not to control directly all that happens in such a way as to suspend or abrogate human freedom and causality. Systematic theologians would say that God's omnipotence is qualified in such a way as to respect human freedom and sustain an orderly world. Therefore, some events occur in the world that are not God's will in a direct sense.

However, it is important for the preacher to remember that this kind of theoretical discussion is seldom helpful in sermons preached amid the emotion of sudden or premature death. After the heat of grief has cooled, and prolonged reflection becomes possible again, some mourners will be helped by a discussion of God's will in a fallen world.

### Preparing to Preach

How should angry questions be handled homiletically? Should the funeral sermon attempt to deal with the question, *why?* Determining how pressing that query really is constantly challenges the pastoral sensitivity of the minister. Are the mourner's anger and related questions a passing phase of grief, real enough, but replaced in a few days or weeks with other feelings? Or is hostility deep and intricate? Will quiet conversation be the best means to deal with the hostility, or will public acknowledgment of the issue serve a positive purpose for the family as well as the broader worshiping congregation? No rules can be given to assist pastors to decide in specific situations. Preachers who err on the side of dealing with anger directly in funeral sermons are constantly surprised by the number of persons who report that the sermon "spoke to them." A pastoral sixth sense that comes only with experience will be your best guide.

One thing should not be done. Published funeral sermons of the past forty years abound with examples of preachers attempting to squelch anger at God. Because each death was viewed, in some sense, as God's will, the loss was perceived by mourners as God's no. Sensing survivors' anger, preachers counseled submission to the absolute sovereign.

> All in all, there is too much murmuring at these occasions. So many seem to find fault. They feel that their mother or father or loved one has died all too soon. . . . God does not make mistakes.[6]

The inherent difficulty of speaking about a loving God who nevertheless causes accidents and slays children surely struck these ministers and priests. Yet expressions of anger by their parishioners were asserted to be sinful evidence of a lack of faith.

The preacher should be very circumspect in speaking about the will of God. Funeral sermons prepared earlier in this century did not hesitate to identify God as the direct cause of all deaths. Death was not simply a boundary for God's created beings, or even the result of sin generally, but death was said to be God's direct will in specific cases. In asserting that God, rather than blind chance or impersonal fate, controls the world, these preachers too easily included specific fatal accidents and childhood tragedies in God's plan for the universe.

But preachers are not perfectly attuned to God's will. Blunt statements that God willed this or that death presume inside knowledge of God. Yet, as Paul reminded us, in this time before faith is turned to sight all believers see but dimly. We know only in part.

Therefore, rather than get into the thorny problem of God's hand in this or that death, preachers should begin by assisting mourners to acknowledge and express the anger they feel. Psychologically, it is probably helpful when blame can be articulated in the sermon. Hortatory appeals to stifle anger actually increase both the anger and guilt of mourners. Giving vent to hostility, or having the preacher express that feeling on behalf of mourners, can free sufferers to voice their own lament.

> What kind of God sits idly by while tragedy—the most unfair kind—takes its toll? What kind of God is that?[7]

The first reaction to this public lament in sermon form may be shock. It seems irreverent. But this may be followed almost immediately by a sense of relief. The unspeakable has been spoken. The preacher's words give permission to sensitive persons to vent similar feelings. Even a cursory reading of the Psalms brings us into the presence of sufferers berating God, who in the end are able to affirm God's goodness and faithfulness.

Thus, by identifying with mourners in their anger, the preacher reassures the bereaved that God will hear their cries. Knowing that a God powerful enough to calm the storm is loving enough to absorb angry questions can be comforting to someone whose world is in collapse. It is important for Christians to know that God can "take it," even when their anger is misdirected.

Then, having acknowledged their anger and having assisted mourners to articulate *why*, the preacher can, without evasion, first shift the response to human causes and afterward introduce God's loving intention for God's people. Pointing to infection, cancer, or heart failure (yes, even suicide) as the cause of death assists mourners to face reality. At the same time, by shifting the focus from God's will to human causes, listeners are prepared for the hopeful message that God in Christ overcame death, that God is with them in the darkness of loss, that God will accompany them through the long night of grief and out into the sunshine of a brighter day.

### What Did I Do to Deserve This?

Guilt seems to be a normal part of grief resulting from loss through death. Paul Tournier reminds us that "there is no grave beside which a flood of guilt feelings does not assail the mind."[8] Self-condemnation seems to result from a clash of emotions that cannot be reconciled at the moment. To be sure, some personality types are more prone to this kind of suffering. But generally speaking, at the death of a loved one some guilt is felt by everyone.

Fear of losing an important person is often felt as guilt. When people upon whom we depend die, fear and guilt are so mingled that they are felt as the same emotion.

Self-reproach may not be realistic. Imagined errors around the selection of a physician or hospital are a common cause of concern after death. "*If only* I had insisted on a second opinion before the operation." "*If only* we had taken him to City General where they do five resections every day." In point of fact, the choice of the doctor, hospital, or treatment may have had nothing to do with the end result, and the decision may have been out of the mourner's hands, but in the mind's eye there is a direct connection between the decision and the death.

Sometimes unrealistic guilt is the result of scapegoating by family members. People tend to blame each other when things go wrong. In the first wave of grief, mourners seek *persons* who are responsible; later on they are better able to discuss *causes*. Decisions that don't turn out right are projected onto others, and self-reproach results when sensitive people take these charges to heart.

Another form of irrational guilt is felt by survivors of accidents or disasters. "Why did I make it, when so many others died?" Survivor guilt is complicated when those killed are younger or perceived as more valuable to society or their families.

In the bewilderment of loss mourners are often unable to distinguish wish and act. Feelings of relief at the death of an aged and suffering parent quickly turn to guilt. If the death has actually been wished, as in the case of a terminally ill and suffering spouse, guilt is complicated further. Although there is no causal relationship between wishing a person's death and the actual death, guilt is keenly felt.

Social expectations at the time of the funeral can complicate guilt further. If standard emotional displays (e.g., crying, kissing the dead) are not performed because of ambivalent feelings, guilt is increased. Ironically, guilt will not be avoided if an expected role is played out of social pressure, and the appropriate feelings are absent.

Often, however, guilt does have a realistic source. No relationship is perfect. There are always things done and left undone. Words of affection that should have been spoken are not; words of condemnation best left unsaid are blurted out in the heat of anger. The final stroke of death eliminates the possibility for forgiveness and reconciliation; guilt is the result.

Sometimes a mourner's inability to carry out the final wishes of the deceased complicates this guilt. A father asks to die at home, but his daughter is unable to care for him there. Thus his death precipitates a flood of guilt. "If only I had tried harder to keep Dad with us." The final wishes of the deceased may be unwise or unfair, but guilt is still felt if those wishes are not fulfilled.

The suffering that accompanies death has a way of taking the issue of guilt to a theological level. Bereaved persons ask, "What did I do to *deserve* this?"

Particularly when a loved one lingers to a cruel death the suffering seems out of all proportion to wrongs known or imagined. In comparison to others whose lives abound with flagrant sins, a believer's suffering (and that of family and friends) appears a gross inequity. The conviction that in this life God rewards the good and causes the evil to suffer is a myth that dies slowly.

So when the guilt of a bereaved person is translated in the question, What did I do to deserve this? a salvation-by-works mentality may barely be disguised. When the sufferer questions God's justice, the assumption may be that the individual has *earned* more equitable treatment. Dynamically, guilt questions may be a natural concomitant to a shallow view of sin.

In digging deeper the pastor may discover a distorted sense of responsibility. Frequently Christians have the feeling that they can and must *do* something in order to control each situation. Persons accustomed to taking charge, those responsible for the care of the dead person, may want to believe that something they did or failed to do caused the death. This can be a subtle form of "playing God."

### Preparing to Preach

When should guilt become a major focus of the funeral message? When self-blame is expressed openly by key mourners, or when the issue of God's justice is raised forcefully, the pastor may decide that guilt is serious enough to address homiletically. When conversations are laced with if only statements, or when decisions made or unmade are rehearsed repeatedly, a mourner may be censuring himself or herself. When the deceased is idealized to the point that negative or painful thoughts about him or her go unrecognized or are angrily rejected, guilt may be the cause. Random displays of temper or outright hostility directed at the deceased or projected to other mourners can be further symptoms. While sermons dealing with guilt may not be pleasant listening for mourners they seldom miss the mark, because guilt is a part of grief for almost everyone.

Helping mourners to understand what they are feeling, by labeling the emotion, should be an aim of funeral sermons focusing on guilt. Most people do not understand that guilt is a phase of grief. They will appreciate hearing that what they are experiencing is normal. An open acknowledgment of the presence of guilt actually enables listeners to begin to confront the affect.

Helping mourners to understand why they feel guilty may be a task for pastoral care rather than for funeral preaching. People often feel remorse for guilt they can identify in order to mask more profound guilt they cannot name. Extended counseling may be necessary to explore the depths of guilt. Even if root causes are known in specific cases these should not become the subject of public sermons.

As has been stated, a funeral sermon is not the place for a detailed analysis of the problem of suffering and its attendant questions of human worthiness and God's justice. Sunday sermons should address dimensions of this issue regularly.

Preachers can assist mourners to deal with guilt by encouraging the remembering process. Positive memories of the deceased are a resource for doing grief work. Verbalizing wholesome experiences with the lost one assists mourners to enthrone these memories in the mind as a partial antidote for guilt.

For mourners afflicted with a distorted sense of responsibility, the good news of the gospel is that they can "let God be God." Having made the decisions that seemed right at the time, and having done their best (inadequate as that might have been), mourners can surrender supreme control of their own lives and those of their loved ones to God. Like the weak and dying Christ, the bereaved can be invited to commend themselves to God's care. When a loved one dies, and slights can no longer be corrected nor human forgiveness sought, God offers the promise of a new beginning.

The assurance that God does forgive sin and assuage guilt can be proclaimed unambiguously. When Paul became a Christian a part of the earliest credal tradition passed on to him was the affirmation "Christ died for our sins" (1 Cor. 15:3). The correlate of the statement that Christ died "for us," which Paul stressed again and again, is the utter inability of human beings to achieve salvation for themselves. Therefore the forgiveness of sin and removal of guilt are always God's gift (Rom. 3:24), always effective "while we were yet sinners" (Rom.

5:8). The action of God precedes our action, our effort, our doing. The "word of the cross" is that the unaccountable are accepted for Jesus' sake. Even in the face of death, this good news can be preached joyfully.

However, the preacher should be cautioned that to proclaim forgiveness before guilt has been acknowledged could be premature. Reassurance prior to confession may serve to deepen guilt and cheapen grace. If pastoral conversation prior to the funeral has not led to an open acknowledgment of guilt feelings, or if there has not been time to clarify them prior to the worship service, the sermon could acknowledge the presence of guilt feelings but take another issue as its main focus. On the other hand, acknowledged or not, it may be the pastor's best judgment that issues of guilt or shame are so pressing that they demand to be addressed directly and immediately.

When the specific word of forgiveness seems premature, God's message of love is an appropriate response to persons whose lives have been shaken. In the midst of self-blame, God's acceptance can be reinforced. God affirms believers as God's children, God's people, part of God's body the church.

The theology of the cross can be helpful to sufferers who understand that God loves and forgives them but who do not feel God's embrace. This theology asserts that believers are tempted daily to fall back into sin. Thus pangs of guilt or feelings of abandonment may be evidence of an ongoing struggle by mourners to become in fact what they already are in promise—forgiven.

Finally, preachers need to remember that forgiveness is God's work. Ministers want to "make it happen" in people's lives, but all they can do is announce the good news of forgiveness in Jesus the Christ. Timothy Lull reminds us that "a central part of the ministry of forgiveness is a waiting on God, a letting people come to faith by their own road, a planting of the seed, and allowing God to give the growth—if growth is to come."[9]

### God, Where Are You?

Depression is a common symptom of loss. It can appear early, within hours or days of a loved one's death. Depression hits frequently when a dying person has lingered in the terminal condition for months, and when family members have worn themselves out in caring for the individual.

Dependent persons may be prone to depression. Mourners who have a history of being unable to deal with difficulties in their own lives feel acutely the loss of someone upon whom they depended. Paradoxically, self-proclaimed independent persons who are threatened by feelings of helplessness are prime targets for spells of depression when their walls of sufficiency shatter under the impact of loss.

Symptoms of depression are legion. People experience feelings that range from mild sadness to profound despair. A lack of activity, inattention to what is going on around them, and self-absorption are prevalent. The common perception of depression is that people sit detached, speaking only when spoken to, and are given to periods of weeping. This is frequently true.

What pastors often miss is that blame can be a prominent part of the total picture. Depressed persons hold themselves responsible for all that has gone wrong in their lives. Or depression expresses itself as anger, often in the form of bitter accusations against the dead person, members of the family, caregivers, or God. At the heart of most depression is a lethal combination of anger-guilt feelings. Because this anger-guilt combination is difficult to express, it is frequently turned inward upon the self as depression.

Degrees of depression may be a clue to the severity of inner turmoil. David Switzer indicates that "the deeper the depressive reaction is in bereavement, the more one would suspect a strong ambivalent conflict and a high degree of guilt."[10]

Diminished self-respect may accompany depression. The bereaved feel humiliated and deprived by their loss. Self-esteem is fragile and easily damaged. The anger-guilt combination may leave the griever feeling like a failure.

Several reactions are possible. Low self-esteem can lead to self-punishing behavior. Mental anguish or self-blame has the side effect of getting attention from others, and may therefore be part of a regressive pattern that takes the bereaved back to a childlike mode of relating. Guilt seems to need punishment, even if it must be self-inflicted.

Self-justifying behavior is another possible response. A guilty person with low self-esteem may retell the story of the death again and again

with himself or herself as the hero. The dead person is idealized exces-
sively, or the relationship between mourner and deceased is exaggerated in a positive way. It is almost as if the bereaved is trying to
convince both the world and the self that he or she is OK.

Withdrawal may be the mourner's way of dealing with anger-guilt
and low self-esteem. The mourner does not want to be disturbed.
While this lassitude is seen as a symptom of depression, it can also be a
positive way of coping. The grieving person is conserving the energy
needed to maintain a low level of functioning and to adapt to the loss.

Finally, helplessness is a sign of depression. The sufferer feels weak
and feeble. A husband is dead, and the widow appears to give up. An
only child dies, and the key to a father's life is gone. Yet helplessness is
both a sign that life has hit bottom and a cry for help. Periods of weeping and evident helplessness say both "I give up" and "I want to live
again."

The pastor-preacher needs to recognize these signs of depression
while at the same time resisting the temptation to exhort mourners to
"snap out of it." If a mourner cannot take the time to vent anger or
withdraw now, mourning can be short-circuited. Feelings that have
not been worked through adequately are apt to surface later in the
same or distorted forms. In both counseling and preaching a pastor
can clue mourners that tolerating each other's unpleasant feelings and
repulsive actions can be the most loving kind of ministry.

"God, where are you?" Generations of believers have put the question this way in the face of death. Mood swings are common for
mourners at various stages of grief. One day the person is optimistic,
hopeful, and confident of surviving the disaster. The next day, or
moment, the same individual is pessimistic and despairing. In the
midst of these fluctuations, whenever God seems absent the cry is
heard, "God, where are you?"

Pastors must be careful not to assume that periods of depression, loss
of faith, and experiences of God's absence are necessary correlates.
While bouts of depression following loss may well be periods when
trust in God wanes, and while hopeful periods are marked frequently
by new bursts of faith, this is not always the case. Depressed persons
often give verbal clues when God seems out of touch.

The experience of God's absence is painful to those who struggle to experience the living Word of God. The more precious that Word, the more acutely will its absence be felt. To the unbeliever, God's silence is normal. For the believer, the breakdown of communication is tragic.

Insofar as Christian mourners are sinful and tempted to doubt and despair, God may seem both absent and enemy. God is not only silent but hostile. God's silence is interpreted as punishment, God's turning away as condemnation.

### Preparing to Preach

Regrettably, many funeral sermons state categorically that mourners should not feel abandoned by God. Of course, urging people to deny honest feelings serves to increase their guilt. Sermons should admit that a descent into doubt and despair is a normal dynamic of faith. Christians who do feel abandoned need not fear that they have committed an unpardonable sin. Knowing the prevalence of feelings of forsakenness, and realizing that dark nights of doubt can be psychic reflexes generated by loss, will reassure depressed mourners.

The recognition of mourners' negative feelings in sermons is a place to begin. But there are other weapons against depression. Waiting is one.

To counsel waiting will not be a trumpet of hope to mourners. Grief-related depression seems interminable. Day follows empty day. Some are a bit brighter and more hopeful than others, but life seems generally devoid of movement. Nothing seems to happen. Nothing seems to change. Frustrated, the mourner cries, "I can't wait any longer!"

So often the tone of voice suggests that waiting is an inadequate response to loss and the feeling of God's absence. But waiting in hope is at the opposite pole from resignation. It involves effort, hard work, and struggle.

The theology of the cross affirms the need for believers to wait, trusting in the action of God. In Christ, the believer receives the forgiveness of sins and becomes a new person. At the same time the Scriptures affirm that believers remain lifelong sinners. For the believer who is simultaneously saint and sinner, waiting between the "already" of Baptism into Christ and the "not yet" of the new being, waiting in obedience is part of what it means to be faithful.

This active waiting exhibits trust in the promise of God. It involves placing confidence in those who heard the Word in the past. When the promise seems unfulfilled and God is silent, the hope is that the Word spoken and heard before will sound forth again. Waiting becomes a persistent call to God to speak. Jacques Ellul writes:

> Hence, in a sense, it could be said that hope is blasphemous. It actually rejects the decision of God's silence. It refuses to give in to the new situation in which God has placed man.[11]

Thus active waiting can take the form of prayer that calls on God to break the silence and reveal God's presence.

Counseling prayer in a funeral sermon may appear to be another weak and futile tack. To many, prayer is a last resort. "When all else fails, pray."

Yet prayer helps mourners to see themselves realistically. In lament they cry out in anger and pain. In confession, fear and guilt surface. In depression, feelings of abandonment are clear. Prayer reveals to sufferers their plight.

At the same time, prayer is an indication that mourners refuse to accept that state of affairs. The incongruity between the helplessness of loss and God's promise of new life and joy issues in a cry to God. Such prayer takes the form of a knock on closed doors. When heaven seems shut and bolted, prayer sets up an urgent tapping. The disparity between God's promise of presence and the closed door provokes an insistent pounding.

Because the not yet is based on promise rather than realization, persistence is required. Mourners should be told this honestly. Persistence is a posture appropriate to a time between the times, to a time of depression, when someone who has heard the Word of God waits to hear again.

Mourners will understand that persistence is impossible without hope. It was, after all, "the sufferings of this present time" that raised Paul's eyes to "the glory that is to be revealed" (Rom. 8:18). The promise that "God will wipe away every tear from their eyes" (Rev. 7:17) keeps grieving persons waiting in hope.

Even as suffering believers wait for God to act God draws near to them in love. We have said that in suffering the cross of Jesus Christ and that of believers can coalesce. There is a mystery to this experience that defies rational explanation. But somehow, in moments of despair, a past event of redemption can become an experience of the crucified and risen Lord. Mourners who cry out to empty skies frequently find another sufferer who can ease feelings of abandonment.

Jesus *was* abandoned by God. Mark's Gospel, the earliest written account, records the cry of dereliction, "My God, my God, why hast Thou forsaken me?" (Mark 15:34). It was for us that God gave Jesus up to death. In Mark's view, Jesus died cut off from God, utterly alone. But because he died that way, we can experience the crucified and risen Lord in the midst of our suffering.

In funeral sermons it is probably a mistake to speak of this as an immediate event. By not taking the mourners' experience of God's absence seriously, and by resorting to hasty reassurance, preachers do not allow grieving persons to experience the absence fully. While God *seems* to be concealed beneath pain and death in order to be found there by those in need, that joyous reunion may be weeks or months away.

It is far better for the preacher to point to means by which God can encounter the depressed. Jesus the Word is the content of various forms of the Word. In the written Word of the Bible, in the Word preached, and in the visible Word of the sacraments, the healing presence of the Lord is made known.

In Baptism God adopts believers into the church. Throughout tension-filled lives, and especially in times of loss and grief, believers return to that covenant and remember what God did for them. As they struggle to "grow up into Christ," God's decision for them in Baptism remains their firm assurance.

In preaching the suffering God comes to sufferers inviting them into a relationship. By virtue of his resurrection, the crucified Christ is present in the preaching of his gospel of forgiveness and new life.

Holy Communion is another form of the Word for helpless mourners. Without the Word, this liturgy remains a ritual meal of bread and wine; with the Word, the meal becomes a sacrament. Through this meal-sacrament God nourishes the helpless and gives them strength for their journey. The Christ of Good Friday and Easter is present and available to believers. At the same time, this meal set in time and space looks forward to the Lamb's high feast, when the saints of every time

and place will sit down with Abraham, Isaac, and Jacob in the kingdom of God.

So in a time of persistent waiting, a time between the times, prayer,
preaching, Baptism, and the Eucharist are a few of the means by
which the crucified God comes to those who ask, "God, where are
you?"

### What Happens at Death—And Beyond?

Death is an experience of chaos that fractures believers intellectually, emotionally, and in terms of decision making. When life seems to
fall apart, people's thoughts, feelings, and judgment go awry. Death
often brings utter confusion along.

For this reason death inspires deep anxiety. This writer accepts "separation anxiety" as an inclusive label to identify what results when one
person loses another through death. Thus the emotions of anger, guilt,
and depression are related to this loss-induced anxiety.

While every loss event within time calls attention to passage—a
child is grown; a relationship is changed—death's loss forces a deeper
confrontation between unconscious timelessness and the reality of lim-
its. Death's loss brings a mourner's sense of immortality face to face
with finitude. The loss is compounded. The survivor loses both a loved
one and his or her own endless life. Anxiety is the alarm system that
sounds when this infinite time is destroyed.

Alarm reactions indicate that a person is aroused by danger to
defense by fight, flight, or freezing. Physical symptoms include rapid
breathing, increased heart rate, muscular tension, dryness of mouth,
and disorders of the gastrointestinal system. Episodes of crying, confusion, and insomnia are commonplace. The alarm has sounded, and
some defensive reaction is instinctive. Even an unnatural calm may
disguise the churning anxiety.

Two particular symptoms of anxiety are of particular importance
for the pastor-preacher. Both searching behavior and bargaining may
contribute to raising questions about death and life beyond death.

Searching behavior is a reaction to loss. When a child runs away
from home, or a married couple separates, the drive to retrieve the lost
one is natural. On the face of it, the search for a dead person is irrational. Yet the search goes on.

Researchers at the University of Minnesota found in a study of bereavement in sixty-six cultures that in almost every case people tend to perceive something like the ghost of the person who has died. These experiences, depending on the culture, can be found gratifying and reassuring or, as in the American culture, may be frightening because people think it means they are losing their minds.[12]

Since searching for the lost person is a powerful reaction to death it may well trigger faith questions in mourners.

Bargaining may do the same. Elisabeth Kübler-Ross identified bargaining as the third stage of anticipatory grief in dying patients.[13] When angry pleas to God have no effect, terminal patients, like children, turn to asking for favors. Bargaining is an attempt to relieve pain, postpone death, or win eternal life. It may well be that bargaining for one's life or the life of the deceased raises into consciousness questions like, "What happens at death—and beyond?"

What does happen at death? In chapter 15 of his first letter to the church at Corinth Paul seems to be challenging one aspect of that congregation's "enthusiasm." Along with their general position that the kingdom had already come in its fullness, the Corinthians evidently imagined death to be essentially behind them. Paul, on the other hand, stressed an order and time sequence. Christ is the "first fruits" of the victory over death. He is alive. But believers will experience resurrection only "at his coming" (v. 23), at "the end" (v. 24). Thus both the futurity of the resurrection and the power of death are underscored.

Paul never promised that death would be avoided. For him the human being is essentially a unity. The word "body" *(sōma)* normally designates the whole person (sometimes the whole person seen negatively, e.g., 1 Cor. 9:27). The person does not have a body; he or she is a body. Likewise "soul" *(psychē)* designates the whole person. Thus there is no suggestion in Pauline literature that the soul, as an independent part of the person, survives and cheats death.

Paul strongly linked sin and death. The reality of physical death is an indication to the apostle that God's creatures have distorted and broken the relationship with their Creator. Symbolically, death represents the extent of human alienation from God, "the wages of sin" (Rom. 6:23).

To be sure, Christ's victory over death embraces his people. In Baptism believers die and rise with him (Rom. 6:1–4). But this eschatological reality does not negate the biological reality of death. "For as in Adam all die, so also in Christ shall all be made alive" (1 Cor. 15:22). The tense of the resurrection promise remains future. Death is one of the hostile powers that is deadly active in the present eon. But eventually this "last enemy" too will be destroyed (1 Cor. 15:26).

Unfortunately, from at least the end of the second century, a large number of believers accepted the dogma, rooted in Greek philosophy and Gnosticism, that the soul is immortal. In the *Phaedo*, Plato asserted that persons are a union of body and soul that is dissolved at death. The body is destroyed but the soul, preexistent and postexistent, continues. This generally accepted belief was formally defined as church doctrine by the Fifth Lateran Council (1512–17).

The result of this understanding is that death appears neither calamitous nor final. The soul, as the unchanging kernel of life at the center of the individual, remains essentially untouched by death. Medieval theology taught that the souls of the dead were already enjoying bliss with God, waiting only for reunion with their glorified bodies on the last day.

The opposite of body/soul dualism would seem to be the view that at death the whole person is obliterated. Death is a devastating reality because the entire person is destroyed.

Therefore anxiety is an understandable response to death. As the German theologian Helmut Thielicke insists:

> The terror of death to which men are sensitive in the Bible does not reside in any anxiety about being roasted in some other-worldly hell. . . . No, the terror of death resides in the fact that here man is simply a totality and therefore in death is totally dead. [14]

Total annihilation is an ominous threat.

This severity is compounded when we realize that before God the individual is unique and irreplaceable. Not only does the individual die, but the individual who dies is one personally loved and valued by God.

There are, of course, various mediating positions between these extremes, but a discussion of these raises a second appropriate question that might be of concern to anxious mourners.

What happens beyond death? It is with God's promises that a discussion of life beyond death should begin. God promises a relationship of love that endures, and this promise is the foundation of the Christian hope.[15] God has revealed love for people in various ways, but especially in the cross of the suffering Christ. The cross event is the basis of the Christian hope. In exposing the Son to suffering and death, God made the commitment to God's people incarnate. What is immortal is not the isolated human soul but our relationship with God. This relationship endures beyond the grave as an eternal expression of the love of God that death cannot destroy.

God promises a relationship of love that endures, and this promise is the substance of the Christian hope. That is to say, the content of promises about the future can be summed up in the word "God." In faith that sees but dimly, and on the basis of revelation that speaks in a variety of images, the one thing we can claim with certainty is that the future is God's future. We belong to God. God has made us God's own in Baptism. On the other side of death God will keep the promise of an eternal relationship of love.

As preacher-theologians, if we say this much and no more about what lies beyond death we are probably on safe ground. In a theology of the cross perspective it is better to say too little than too much. On this side of death both sight and knowledge are imperfect (1 Cor. 13:12). Two things alone are certain; death is real and final, and beyond death our hope is in God. God created us out of nothing, and remembering us in love, God is able to do that again.

### Preparing to Preach

What happens at death? In ministry to persons who have suffered the loss of a loved one, pastors are struck at how seldom the question is posed. The carefully rehearsed speeches of pastors go unused. Perhaps the anxiety of mourners is being hidden, or at least questions stifled, in order to avoid threatening clergy. Ministers and priests need to encourage mourners to articulate their pressing questions.

During ten years of parish ministry it was heartening for this writer to discover that most grieving people did seem able to accept death's reality. The majority of Christians were ready to deal with loss head-on. Therefore, precisely because most mourners seem willing to accept it, preaching about the reality and finality of death should not go out of its way to be offensive. Honesty does not depend upon lurid descriptions of decay.

It aids reality to speak of death as a "last enemy" (the Pauline characterization) rather than as a natural friend. For believers who remain sinners, death is seldom viewed as a helpful process of disposal. Even when persons wish for the approach of death, or pray for it, the end of life has a tragic quality. False heroism in the face of death is inappropriate. Victory over death is Christ's first of all, and ours only as an undeserved gift. By admitting the antagonistic nature of death, preachers help listeners face death's reality.

Again, references to God's agency in causing or permitting death contribute to a denial of death's own power. Using words like cancer, heart attack, and stroke in the sermon help to bring death "down to earth."

It is perfectly proper in the sermon to refer to the survivors' own emotional confrontations with mortality. Death has already reminded mourners of a barrier beyond which they cannot go. However, it seems to this writer that citing death as a warning to repent and believe preys on the emotions of mourners when they are most vulnerable and, therefore, constitutes irresponsible manipulation. Preaching about the threat of hell at funerals is inexcusable.

Finally, it is important in the sermon to acknowledge that death severs relationships. Mourners are separated from the deceased physically, although images of the dead person can be helpfully integrated into their memory systems. The chain of broken relationships extends beyond the immediate family circle to neighbors, friends, and brothers and sisters in Christ. These severed bonds can be acknowledged. Sermonic stress on the theme of brokenness combined with a deemphasis of the theme of reunion will assist mourners to accept death as a true terminus, an important prelude to the rebirth of life and hope.

"What happens beyond death?" Pastors report that mourners seldom raise this question directly. In my early years of parish ministry I found the silence puzzling. Gradually I came to realize that many lay persons were accepting the biblical imagery of heaven as picture language that even the pastor could not decipher. These Christians were concerned primarily with their own loss and seemed content (most of the time) to place their loved ones in the keeping of a God whose promise they trusted.

Nevertheless, as soon as the preacher chooses language to enflesh and elaborate that promise, difficulties begin. While the language of immortality was the choice of church fathers to stress the preservation of the individual self, that metaphor is not helpful today. It appears to deny the reality and discontinuity of death. The terminology of immortality suggests that, like God, humans continue to "be" through and beyond death. Yet God alone possesses the sort of "life" that endures. We can receive it only as a gift. Even if it is said that immortality is a gift of God, in common parlance the idiom denies death.

The language of resurrection has the benefit of being Hebraic and solidly biblical. Further, it takes death seriously as the end of life—no created thing cheats death. The link between Easter Day and the fate of believers is clear. God raised Jesus from the dead and "will also raise us by his power" (1 Cor. 6:14). The terminology of resurrection is compatible with the concept of a re-creation of the whole person. The New Testament suggests that a believer's total life and being will be transformed by the risen Christ "to be like his glorious body" (Phil. 3:21).

Still, the preacher must be aware that resurrection language too is metaphorical and that it does not communicate self-evidently in this culture.[16] Therefore, contemporary images must be found to supplement the Bible's standard fare.

While metaphors from everyday life can be helpful, some traditional metaphors present more problems that others. Reunion language, for example, may say more than the Bible itself permits about future relations with dead loved ones. C. S. Lewis reminds us that "reality never repeats."[17] Pictures of family reunions on the other side of death are apt to be taken too literally by mourners, imposing a shape on eternal life that is really God's to design.

Because the term "heaven" has been associated with graphic (and fanciful) descriptions of reunion, the preacher may choose to limit its use in preaching. Obviously, care should be taken in hymn selection to avoid the kind of "gospel songs" that paint heaven as one big Sunday-school picnic protracted eternally.

The biblical metaphor of "rest" or "sleep" may still be helpful as a pointer to the condition of believers after death. The image suggests both the peaceful and the ephemeral nature of their state. Luther spoke in a graphic way of waking up from sleep "in Christ."

> We are to sleep until He comes and knocks on the grave and says, "Dr. Martin, get up." Then I will arise in a moment and will be eternally happy with Him. [18]

This metaphor is also helpful in dealing with the time problem of a resurrection to judgment that Scripture seems to speak of as both immediate and future. While sleep may be prolonged from the observer's point of view, to the sleeper it passes like the snap of a finger.

One weakness of rest and sleep metaphors is their inability to express the seriousness and finality of death. They have the further disadvantage of suggesting the question, Where do the dead sleep? In itself the image does imply an intermediate state, but it need not lead to a fully developed doctrine of purgatory. The canonical Scriptures themselves resist this temptation.

To say that a believer is held "in God's memory" has the advantage of stressing the reality of death. This is akin to the process of introjection by which the dead person is "resurrected" in the memory of friends and loved ones. However, the phraseology should be avoided if listeners are apt to believe "that's all there is." In fact, some contemporary theologians suggest that what survives death is *not* the person but "the eternal presence of his/her earthly life within the divine memory." [19] In this view, after death God remembers believers and brings their lives to fruition in making effective their contribution to the kingdom of God. Therefore, in the use of memory *and* resurrection language together the collective image of memory is at least susceptible to the understanding of human reformation that is in some sense individual.

In the end, the everyday metaphor of "reconciliation with God" may be the most helpful image. It has the advantage of taking seriously the break in the God relationship that sin and death imply. Further, reconciliation is a joyful human experience. Stories of reconciliation in daily life may be employed by the preacher as images of what is to come.

> To be saved from death means to be set free for a new relationship to God and for a new relationship to oneself. This involves that the threat which

we ourselves imagine we must meet at the end of our lives has lost its power, that the curse of those actions which cause us to lose and forfeit our lives is broken. . . . Salvation from death means therefore that we are set free *both* to live *and* to die.[20]

Most important, since ministers and priests preach to mourners and not to the deceased, and since new life now rather than resurrection after death is of prime concern to listeners, the metaphor of reconciliation can link present and future in the sermon. If death is "an impulse toward relationlessness" (Jungel) involving separation from loved ones (loss) and from God (alienation), then reconciliation with God is a gift that for believers can begin now under the medium of biological life and can be consummated beyond death.

In the end we are really saying that every metaphor is flawed. The best conceal as well as reveal. The worst distort more than they clarify. The preacher is charged with employing the most apt images available to communicate to specific listeners as well as with using images in sufficient variety to offset the weaknesses of each. In this way ministers and priests have a chance to break through the roadblocks grief erects. After all, what we point to now in language may not yet be fully planned by God. Some surprises await us!

> For the trumpet will sound,
> and the dead will be raised . . . ,
> and we shall be changed.
> (1 Cor. 15:52)

## NOTES

1. Douglas John Hall, *Lighten Our Darkness: Toward an Indigenous Theology of the Cross* (Philadelphia: Westminster Press, 1976), 150.

2. Ibid., 113.

3. C. S. Lewis, *A Grief Observed* (New York: Seabury Press, 1963; New York: Bantam, 1976), 35.

4. *Luther's Works*, Vol. 31 (Philadelphia: Fortress Press, 1957), 40.

5. Eberhard Jungel, *Death: The Riddle and the Mystery*, trans. Iain Nicol and Ute Nicol (Philadelphia: Westminster Press, 1974), 59–80.

6. R. R. Belter, *To Die Is Gain* (Burlington, Vt.: Lutheran Literary Board, 1951), 65.

7. *Through the Valley of the Shadow* (Lima, Ohio: C.S.S. Publishing Co., 1976), 41.

8. Paul Tournier, *Guilt and Grace* (New York: Harper & Row; London: Hodder & Stoughton, 1962), 93, quoted in David Switzer, *The Dynamics of Grief* (Nashville: Abingdon Press, 1970), 131.

9. Timothy Lull, "Weariness with Our Basic Task," *LCA Partners* (April 1981): 15.

10. Switzer, *Dynamics of Grief*, 138.

11. Jacques Ellul, *Hope in Time of Abandonment*, trans. C. Edward Hopkin (New York: Seabury Press, 1973), 178.

12. Bertha Simos, *A Time to Grieve* (New York: Family Service Association of America, 1979), 95.

13. Elisabeth Kübler-Ross, *On Death and Dying* (New York: Macmillan Co., 1969), 82–84.

14. Helmut Thielicke, *Death and Life* (Philadelphia: Fortress Press, 1970), 98.

15. Wolfhart Pannenberg develops clearly the concept of a "promise event" based on the resurrection of Jesus from the dead.

16. Lee E. Snook makes this point in "Death and Hope—An Essay in Process Theology," in *Dialog* 15 (Spring 1976): 126.

17. Lewis, *Grief Observed*, 29.

18. *D. Martin Luther's Werke*. Kritische Gesamtausgabe (Weimar, 1883–) 37, 151, quoted in Althaus, *The Theology of Martin Luther*, trans. Robert C. Schultz (Philadelphia: Fortress Press, 1966).

19. John H. Hick, *Death and Eternal Life* (New York: Harper & Row, 1976), 215–27.

20. Jungel, *Death: The Riddle and the Mystery*, 127.

# 4
# The Funeral Sermon

---

Edgar Jackson said that "the heart of any act is the overcoming of difficulties in the medium for the sake of the meaning."[1] This chapter concentrates on the medium of funeral preaching, and the overcoming of difficulties that have limited its effectiveness in communicating the reality of death and the hope of new life in Jesus Christ. The model for designing funeral sermons projected here will enable the preacher to match specific situations of death with appropriate responses of faith. Even in the midst of darkness God's trumpet of hope can sound.

## THE SCOPE
## OF FUNERAL SERMONS

If asked about the scope of funeral messages, many experienced pastors are quick to reply, "keep it short." Specifically, they favor a sermon in the five- to ten-minute range. Given the mental and physical condition of mourners and their resulting attention span, that may be good advice. Yet length is a minor facet of the question of scope. Indeed, the five- to ten-minute guideline may be violated if conceptually and structurally the sermon is of limited scope.

The funeral message must have concentration if it is to communicate to anxious listeners. Every detail should contribute to the whole. There is no time for exploring bypaths. The funeral sermon is more like the crisp movement of a short story than it is like the leisurely development of a full-length novel.

This means, among other things, that the mood and direction of the message are set from the opening sentence. Introductions are excess baggage. There is no time to explore the half feelings and in-between emotions of every segment of the congregation. While a range of questions may be acknowledged, all but one are left undeveloped. The sermon must have focus.

If carefully done, the sermon sentence embodies the central thrust of the message. John Henry Jowett's is the classic statement on this issue:

> No sermon is ready for preaching, nor ready for writing out, until we can express its theme in a short, pregnant sentence as clear as a crystal. I find the getting of that sentence the hardest, the most exacting, and the most fruitful labor in my study.[2]

For the preacher, the tedium in producing crystalline sentences is rewarded by the elimination of irrelevant ideas and the concentration of amorphous impressions. For the listener, the result should be a unified sermon with one sharp message.

While the task is painstaking, the process for writing sermon sentences is easily explained.[3] A question is useful to spark the effort. In answer to the theological query, What is God doing here? one concise sentence is constructed.

*God* should be the subject of the sentence. Preaching normally centers on God's action, or it is not fit to bear the name. The gospel, particularly the cross-resurrection event, is at the heart of Christian funeral preaching. So the sentence begins with God, or more specifically, with Jesus Christ or the Holy Spirit.

Identify the action next. What is God *doing*? If a biblical pericope is central to the sermon development, then God's action is clear. What God did in the past, the sermon proclaims God is doing in the present. If what God did (in the text) seems irrelevant for these mourners, inappropriate for this funeral message, or somehow invalid for use today, the only option is to get another text or to preach a topical sermon.

Scripture tells us that God understands suffering and pain. God cares for the deceased and mourners. God is on the griever's side, supporting, strengthening, and healing. God suffers when God's people do. God reunites believers to divine fellowship. God recenters lives and reforms what has been shattered. All these and more are God's actions, the present work of a crucified and living Lord in particular loss situations.

God's action always has a particular referent. What is God doing *here*? Attempting to state precisely what God is doing in specific situations is, from one point of view, the height of presumption. Yet knowing who God is (insofar as God has revealed that) and knowing something of what God has done (from the Bible and church history) enables preachers to make prayerful affirmations about what the faithful God is doing right now.

In chapter 1 we came to know Paul, his wife Gwen, and their two daughters, Jennifer and Jill. When Gwen was diagnosed as having lung cancer, Paul's initial reaction was anger. A difficult marriage had become fulfilling. Paul resented death cheating him and Gwen of their life together. However, as the illness dragged on anger was replaced by a feeling of acquiescence in both of them. Both prayed that the suffering would be over. Jennifer felt abandoned. She was an eleven-year-old who needed her mother desperately. Jill, away at college during the months of pain and deterioration, blamed her father for giving up too easily, for his honest admission that he wanted it over. Her own guilt at being unavailable to help compounded the guilt of her father. In the struggle, and in the tense aftermath of death, Paul felt abandoned by God as well.

If constructed carefully, a single declarative sentence can be packed with information. At the same time the writing of that sentence forces the preacher to select a single emotion and/or question to target in the sermon.

In preaching to Paul, Jennifer, Jill, and the other mourners present, the pastor could zero in on tension in the family, the resulting guilt, or the issue of whether or not it is OK to feel relief at the death of a loved one. Instead, because it was felt to be an underlying issue for all three family members, the pastor chose to focus on the theme of abandonment.

The text chosen was Luke 24:13–35, the story of Jesus' encounter with two bereaved disciples on the road to Emmaus that first Easter night. The pastor's summary sentence was:

The risen Christ visited two disciples in the guise of a traveler and, as their meal guest, revealed himself to them, strengthening them.

The sermon sentence took this form.

In the situation of Gwen's cancer death, the risen Christ comes to mourners on their journey, revealing himself in word and meal, and strengthening them in the fellowship of his body the church.

A final important issue is touched in this sermon sentence, namely, the question *How?* In the sentence above, how Jesus comes is answered in two ways. He comes "in word and meal" and "in the fellowship of his body the church." As we shall see, both ideas come from the text that has been chosen and both will be elaborated in the structure and content of the sermon.

## THE STRUCTURE
## OF FUNERAL SERMONS

In most discussions of sermon structure, two opposing tendencies are evident. Some regard sermon form as a kind of empty shell, a preformed mold, to be filled with homiletical content. Others argue that each sermon has its own unique shape, one that grows out of its content.

The preacher who employs fixed sermon models probably saves preparation time. The structure is given. At most the pastor is required to sort through the options available and select the structure that best fits the content. With at least a tolerable fit between form and substance, the minister can invest energy in refining the content of the message.

Of course fixed forms can be awkward and wooden. Content can tax set structures to the breaking point. The sermon message can be distorted by forcing it into an ill-fitting container. As in Jesus' day, new skins may be necessary to carry the sparkling wine of the gospel.

H. Grady Davis defends the position that each sermon must have its own unique form.

> There is a right form for each sermon. . . . A right form can never be imposed on any sermon. If it has to be imposed it is not right. The right form derives from the substance of the message itself, is inseparable from the content, becomes one with the content, and gives a feeling of finality to the sermon.[1]

Each sermon has its own shape, one that its content assumes. Form and substance are inseparable.

However, in seeking the "right form" for each funeral sermon an obvious problem is time. With two days, at most three, between death and funeral, a busy pastor has only a limited time in which to wrestle with text and situation. Structure may not have latitude to evolve.

This writer agrees with the spirit of Davis's position. Yet it need *not* mean that every time a preacher sits down to prepare a funeral sermon he or she makes a totally fresh beginning. Davis himself points the way for us with his statement that "a functional form is a form taken by a thing the better to accomplish its purpose."[5] Rather than sermon forms being vessels of fixed shape into which the content of the gospel is poured, or forms unique to each message, hints for structure are found in the overall "purpose" of a given type of sermon.

### Objectives of the Funeral Sermon

If "form follows function," it may be that the objectives of the funeral sermon can help to give it shape. For Christians these are essentially two: 1. *help mourners face the reality of death*; 2. *assist mourners to discover the hope of new life in Christ*. Of course, a good deal can be said about each function, and what has been said will help us construct subsidiary purposes.[6]

### Help mourners face the reality of death

- By helping mourners to accept both the finality of death and their particular loss.
- By helping mourners to view grief as therapeutic and to engage in the grief process themselves.
- By avoiding euphemisms for death and other mechanisms of denial while embracing images that touch mind and imagination.

### Assist mourners to discover the hope of new life in Christ

- By projecting a vision of God that will be a positive help and comfort to suffering Christians.
- By assisting mourners to see their situations from the perspective of new life grounded in the death and resurrection of Jesus.
- By helping mourners to achieve, proleptically (by anticipation), a vision of personal integration and wholeness.

A score of other functions could be added. Yet it should be clear in the pages that follow that the major structural divisions of the funeral sermon are derived from the purposes above. The objective of helping mourners face the reality of death gives rise to movement 1, Reality: The Situation of Death and Loss; the goal of assisting mourners to discover hope in Christ issues in movement 2, Hope: The Response of Faith. These movements are principal divisions because they are "functional forms" able to accomplish the sermon's purposes.

The choice of terminology is intentional. Speaking of the story of death, the mourners' story, and God's story marks this sermonic approach as essentially narrative. Narrative or story preaching views sermon development as more akin to the plot line of a short story than the point by point outline of classical didactic preaching. In *Story and Reality* Robert Roth notes, "Stories begin once upon a time. They move through episodes to a climax and then come to an end. . . . Stories move. They have a plot."[7] For this reason I will speak of the movements of the funeral sermon rather than of its outline.

Thinking of the funeral sermon as a series of episodes within two major movements of one sermonic plot provides for flexibility. The skilled preacher can interchange and rearrange episodes as necessary. As the playwright breaks a story into scenes, in part to permit flexibility, so a narrative plot structure makes funeral sermons susceptible to rearrangement.

Of course, not every episode is necessary each time, and some can be eliminated. The peaceful death of a ninety-year-old widower may not raise a theological question to be addressed. In most cases of mutilation, the story of death should not be retold in the sermon. The narrative plot design allows the preacher to add or subtract episodes as function and common sense indicate.

Finally, this writer's structural analysis of funeral sermons preached in various Christian traditions during the past forty years has revealed the presence, on a regular basis, of key ingredients. The episodes to be described in this chapter can assist mourners to face reality even as they find hope in Christ.

## PUTTING THE
## FUNERAL SERMON TOGETHER

### First Movement: The Reality of
### Death and Loss

Funeral preaching involves the sensitive juxtaposing and interweaving of three stories: the dead person's, the mourners', and God's. Our discussion begins where the sermon frequently does—with the story of death.

*Make contact by telling the story of death.* The funeral sermon should deal with death realistically. Unless the loss is acknowledged, faced, and accepted the funeral will not provide a sense of finality for mourners. The first movement of the sermon is dedicated to that end.

Beginning with a reference to the deceased is helpful. It is the tact expected by many Christians. Mourners are frequently consumed with thoughts of the dead. As they sit in the quiet of church or funeral establishment minds drift back to the event. Frequently the coffin is open before them. Because listeners are ready to hear about their loved one, the message has a good chance to make contact.

During an initial visit with mourners the story of death is told to the pastor. Now, in the context of proclamation, the preacher tells the story to mourners. On this public occasion retelling the story can put their loss in front of relatives and friends in a way that enables them to acknowledge it. The aim is to convey the experience so that mourners feel—not just know intellectually, but experience—the reality of death.

Preachers should use the dead person's name to avoid a "to whom it may concern" flavor. Significant events and activities of the deceased can be mentioned as appropriate. Recounting these accurately encourages the remembering process that is at the heart of effective grieving. Obviously, graphic descriptions of the person's death are out of place. Eulogizing (in the sense of overpraising) both edges God out of the center of the sermon and impedes mourning. But when the dead person's life and conduct are described without embellishment, a firm sense of reality is established.

*Move to the mourners' stories.* Telling the story of death makes contact with grieving listeners, involves the congregation, and, without eulogizing, encourages the mourning (remembering) process. But the primary focus of attention in the funeral sermon is the survivors. A subtle shift to them and their feelings is in order.

The pastor's story may be appropriate, because ministers and priests are mourners too. From a more or less objective recounting of the death, the preacher may be able to move the sermon to the feeling level by sharing a personal reaction to the loss. Seeing the event through the preacher's eyes, feeling along as his or her feelings are shared, frees mourners to move beyond themselves. This shift of perspective may enable family and friends to see and feel the loss as others do.

In addition, this recounting may save the pastor from the appearance of detached professionalism. While it is true that clergy need to be in control of emotions to conduct the liturgy and preach, the cold detachment they sometimes convey is repulsive to mourners. Sharing feelings with sensitivity and restraint can establish a deep rapport. The family is touched by someone who both feels the loss and testifies to faith's resources for facing it. But again, the lightest touch is essential lest the preacher become the focus.

The congregation's story should be told *if* such a recounting is warranted. If the person was a key leader or faithful member whose death will leave an empty pew, this loss can be acknowledged in the sermon. Of course, any expression of sadness on behalf of the congregation must be genuine. If the impact of the death on the life, work, and emotions of the community is overstated and sounds fabricated, communication will be imperiled.

The family's story is the culmination of the narrative recounting of the event and leads into a focus on the question(s) being asked. The aim of this episode is to help the immediate family and loved ones to come to grips with their own emotions.

Reality is especially important here. The preacher acknowledges the broken family circle. The preacher labels feelings that arise when deep relationships end. If some are angry at God, or feeling guilty, that fact may be noted. A climate for mourning is established by allowing mourners to acknowledge and accept their feelings.

Of course there are dangers. First, the pastor can say too much. She or he may become too personal or reveal family feelings easily linked to individuals. It would be an inexcusable affront to identify specific mourners and their feelings from the pulpit. If people become self-conscious and embarrassed, their own feelings intrude and dialogue suffers. Never say, "George, I know you're feeling guilty," or "Amy, you are angry at God for taking Mike away." Show discretion. "Some of you are feeling guilt over Mike's death; a few may be angry with God for taking him away."

A second problem is created when pastors feel obliged to squelch "negative" feelings, particularly those directed toward God. Urging listeners not to feel what burns inside them is both a flight from reality and ineffective. Furthermore, it functions to increase the very emotion being condemned. Listener guilt or anger may grow as a result of the preacher defending God. Since God does not need human defenders, and since negative emotions are normal for forgiven sinners under stress, preachers would do well to simply acknowledge this.

A third problem is created when pastors suggest that one grief-related emotion is neatly replaced by its successor. The discovery is soon made in parish ministry that the so-called stages of grief are not really stages at all. If only shock, anger, guilt, depression, and acceptance arrived as predictably as telephone poles along a highway, leaving in the exact order of their appearing! Rather, they and their attendant questions tend to occur and recur over a more or less defined period. Faced with this apparent randomness and flux the pastor must be careful not to suggest that a particular feeling will disappear forever.

So, the heightened realism that occurs by telling the story of death from the perspective of various mourners comes to a climax in the family's story. Now the preacher has an opportunity to yoke feeling with cognition, emotions with the questions being asked.

*Focus on one question being asked.* By telling the story of death and recounting the loss from a variety of perspectives the survivors should be in touch with their grief. Now, for the sermon to advance, felt meaning requires symbolization. Verbal clarification is in order.

On the face of it, funeral preaching has no problem with relevance. Death and its ensuing grief are the problems to be addressed. Further, the family of the deceased and the dead person's closest friends are the primary hearers. With good conscience the preacher may focus on them.

Yet the apparent advantage of a narrowly defined audience presents a difficult challenge. The dynamic processes involved in loss leave the listeners, even the immediate family, at different stages of grief with diverse questions.

For example, Paul Olson endured tortuous periods of anger and depression during Gwen's bout with terminal cancer. Yet after nine months of dealing with death by anticipation he seems on the verge of putting his life back together. Paul feels guilty for feeling better; he feels abandoned by God as well. He asks, "Where is God in this darkness?" At the same time, the couple's oldest daughter Jill, nine hundred miles away at college during the illness of her mother, comes to the event without a firsthand experience of her mother's (and father's) pain. She is angry at God for "taking" her mother from her and annoyed that her father's tears have dried. Behind that may be the guilty question, "What if I had taken a semester off and come home?" Her eleven-year-old sister Jennifer, feeling lost and alone in the world, pleads, "How can I live without Mom?"

How is the preacher to address this family when so many different emotion-laden questions are being asked? Picking the most pressing question, while alluding to others, is a structural necessity in a sermon of this scope.

Focusing on one key issue is a process of abstraction. While the term abstraction may have obscure or difficult connotations, this centering process actually simplifies the dialogue between preacher and mourners. As a student uses a yellow marker to highlight the key assertion in a paragraph, so the pastor assists baffled mourners to focus. Shaping the sermonic plot around a single issue gives the minds and emotions of the bereaved a sense of clarity.

Intellectual bafflement is intolerable for most people. Our natures demand that we make sense of life. Yet perceptive individuals know that death's dilemma defies simple solutions. Final answers are not expected. What mourners need from a public response in the midst of a continuing conversation is a frame of reference to help them work on the issue.

By raising many of the feelings and questions represented in the congregation, by acknowledging them as honest and appropriate while focusing on just one, the preacher has the best chance of addressing some persons directly while holding the interest of others. Most people have asked the pressing questions that accompany death. It helps the preacher to know that a pointed question of one mourner may, on another level, haunt all of them.

*Employ an effective image of death or grief.* We said in chapter 1 that images are effective because they express reality in a way different from the way labels and reasoned statements do. "Most people, even educated people, do not listen analytically but are affected by the pattern of imagery in an utterance."[8] Minds work by association, leaping from image to image, rather than by logical point-by-point progression. Thought is immediate, personal, and concrete. Grieving persons, often dazed and confused, find it easier to see pictures than to follow arguments.

In the initial movement of a funeral sermon, the simple image of a car out of control on an icy road disclosed the situation of a middle-aged woman, widowed without warning, far more effectively than minutes of talking about sudden death. When this metaphor was employed by the preacher, the widow was observed jamming the brake to the floor as she was gripped by the image. She simultaneously understood and felt what it meant to be "out of control."

Sometimes the pastor, sensitive to the hobbies, employment, or life style of mourners (or the deceased), can suggest fitting images. To a woman who passed her evenings doing thousand-piece jigsaw puzzles, the metaphor of a completed puzzle suddenly spilled on the floor had insightful meaning. The preacher was able to speak of the grief process as putting a puzzle back together with some pieces missing.

Occasionally an apt image can be reclaimed from a prefuneral visit. When a suddenly widowed parishioner described herself (relating the event to a childhood experience) as a little girl lost among the crowds at a county fair, unable to find her mother's hand, the image was usable in the funeral sermon. In the case we have been following Paul shared with the pastor his recurring dream of waking up in a strange country beside a deserted road. He felt alone, afraid, and uncertain of which direction to go. The pastor will be able to employ that dream as a graphic image of abandonment.

Sometimes images resorted to by mourners are not appropriate for preaching. A mother reported that her son, prior to his suicide, had described himself as a "throw-away milk carton" from which all the contents had been "drained." However, the implications of that vivid image for those present at the funeral who had "drained" him made its use in the sermon inappropriate.

## A Sermonic Sample

Just as images are effective in symbolizing the reality of death in the initial movement of the sermon plot, as the plot develops we will find them communicating the hope of new life. The first movement of the sermon preached by the pastor at Gwen's funeral will be an example of how, in one specific situation, a pastor dealt with the reality of death and loss. The text is Luke 24:13–35. Analysis of the sermon appears in boldface type, set apart from the text by brackets. Please read this first movement of the sermon aloud the first time through, then reread in light of the analysis.

For several months now, those of us who knew Gwen best realized that we would be together on an evening like this. At the beginning, when the doctors first said the dread word cancer, the whole world seemed black as night. But then a candle of hope was lit. The chemotherapy appeared to be working. Gwen was back in the choir and teaching in the third-grade class. The candle burned brightly.

[Use the personal name in telling the story of death.

The term cancer adds a note of reality and focuses on the true cause of death.

Darkness is Paul's own image. The candle is an image of hope.]

Three months ago the flame began to go out. Choir members noticed that the old weariness had returned. It became an effort just to walk down the aisle, and Gwen began slipping into the choir loft through the rear door. Few of you knew of the long nights of pain, of struggles to breathe, of the gradual realization that the battle was coming to an end. Finally, Gwen herself prayed that the struggle would be over.

[Going over the story of Gwen's decline assists mourners to explore their own memories. These memories should speak to Jill, who blames her father for giving up.]

Here at St. John's we will all miss Gwen: her sweet soprano voice, her willingness to listen to those who needed a friend, her commitment to the work of Christ and the church. I will never forget the courage she displayed. When I visited Gwen in the hospital she always asked first about my family and her friends here at St. John's.

[This is clearly a case where the congregation's story of loss and grief should be told. The pastor's story completes the picture and is appropriate. Recounted simply, it does not smack of embellishment.]

I know that a few of you are so stunned by Gwen's death that you are frozen and numb. The thaw will come soon with its flood of tears. Some of you are feeling guilty. You may be asking, "How could I have helped? She helped me so often." Yet my hunch is that right now the most pressing issue is a vague, undefined anger. It may touch the doctors who never seemed to help. Frankly, much of your anger may be directed at God. I've heard several remark, "Why did God allow this to happen to a faithful Christian, a fine mother, a wonderful person?" You are really asking, "Why did God abandon Gwen?" Paul, Jennifer, you sat and watched with Gwen during the agony of her struggle. You may be feeling abandoned too.

[This episode cites a number of emotions while coming to focus on the feeling of anger and the question of divine abandonment. Naming Paul and Jennifer is a calculated risk. Rather than link feelings to particular persons outright, the preacher uses "may" to signal an educated guess.]

Feeling alone is frightening. Sometimes losing someone close is like waking up in a strange country beside a deserted road. You struggle to your feet, uncertain how you got there, not sure which direction to go. The world is empty and silent.

[Paul's image is used without labeling it as his. Because the feelings involved are universal, the image communicates.]

I'm sure the disciples felt that way after Good Friday. They left families and careers to follow Jesus, and nothing came of it. They led their messiah into Jerusalem with palms waving, but he was soon in jail. They risked everything on a promising leader, and he was executed as a common criminal. The leaders of the temple were rumored to be mounting a house-to-house search for the dead man's followers. Some disciples went into hiding. Others left Jerusalem and headed for home. All felt abandoned.

[The move into the biblical text is smooth. A clear identification is made between the first- and twentieth-century mourners.]

### Second Movement: The Good News of the Gospel

Stories often have a point where the action shifts. In literature this may be called a "crux" or "gesture." At this juncture the tale turns in a new direction.

The shift from reality to hope in the sermon is such a juncture. Frequently this occurs in the text where, with the disciples or Mary, we jump from despair to hope, fear to courage, sorrow to joy. Thus the retelling of the biblical story can be the structural transition from the situation of loss and grief to the response of faith.

*Proclaim the good news.* Biblical narratives carry impact, because in them God interacts with God's people. The goal of these stories is commitment and faith. As "witness literature" they not only talk about a God who cares for suffering persons, but they become vehicles for God's gracious approach. Biblical narratives both evoke reality and invoke the God of hope.

The most effective text for funeral sermons is a hinge. At the grave of Lazarus we not only see Jesus weep, but we hear the good news, "I am the resurrection and the life" (John 11:25). In the upper room we not only sense the disciples' fear, but we hear the reassuring, "Peace be with you" (John 20:19). In the midst of these narratives the action shifts from human anguish to God's promise of help. Two different Scripture references can be used, one to mirror reality and the other to proclaim hope. Unfortunately, then the unity given by a single text is lost.

*Focus on the Christ story.* This is one way for the preacher to help mourners resolve the death/life dichotomy. In the Christ story death and life are no longer absolutely opposed. Death can be viewed as the beginning of life (for Christ himself, for us in Baptism). Thus the death/resurrection event of Jesus of Nazareth is the heart of funeral preaching for Christians. The one who really died is alive, and this gospel brings hope for the deceased (resurrection) and for mourners (new life).

*Employ theological clues.* In guiding someone through a period of struggle, clues are essential. Having focused on a specific problem or question, the preacher is tempted to render a simple solution. Unfortunately, that doesn't work. Grief clouds perception. Clarity rarely comes all at once for anyone. Even if the preacher's answer is a good one, listeners may not be able to hear or accept it. Rather, funeral preaching at this point will have the character of a probe. Clues will be offered to lead mourners from one promising path to another. A hint here, a suggestion there, and searchers are enlisted in a quest that may prove fruitful eventually.

A careful analysis of mourner feelings and questions should suggest theological clues that are appropriate. If the disintegration of a trusted relationship is the problem, then the promise of union with Christ within the church may offer solace. If fear is the overriding concern, the courage God supplies is a helpful clue. If doubt presses in, faith is proclaimed as a gift of God. This is done carefully, with a light touch, giving clues rather than insisting what must be believed, in order for suffering faith to find its way to understanding.

It will be well to resist the temptation to probe deeply the great contradictions death raises. Why a loving God permits suffering, for example, is too complex an issue to handle in a brief sermon. It is the kind of problem that deserves a series of sermons or extended pastoral conversation.

Even a superficial reading of books of funeral sermons will reveal some of the false clues preachers give at this point in the sermonic plot. One of the worst is the tendency of some clergy to ascribe particular deaths to God's direct agency. Even if the preacher feels that death is more than a boundary for all created beings, and more than the result of sin generally, speaking of God's will in specific cases is not helpful or honest. At the death of older persons, preachers speak too easily of God's loving will in "calling the faithful home." When suffering is prolonged it is tempting to call death "God's blessing." But trying to be consistent in ascribing fatal accidents and agonizing illnesses to God has caused many mourners to project their anger on God. Stating without reservation that children die because God wants them more than their parents is a particularly sickening example of this mentality. Faith may be destroyed just when mourners need it most.

In addition, the misleading impression is left that the preacher has inside knowledge about God's will in specific cases. If a minister or priest can admit bafflement in the face of tragic death this actually helps mourners. They sense that they are not alone in their feelings. Citing more apparent causes of death (e.g., cancer, heart disease) in the sermon may actually help listeners to establish a firm sense of reality.

When mourners already have theological clues to their situation, the preacher may be able to make use of these. Favorite Scripture passages can be reinforced through use in the sermon.

When a mourner's understanding of death, as revealed in pastoral conversation, is flawed, a fresh alternative may be advanced in the sermon. Neither the integrity of the preacher nor of the church's beliefs is at stake. Rather, sufferers need a perspective on death and life that will enable them to find meaning and hope. If a grieving mother views God as a sadist who kills children, then that individual's anger will impede her return to wholeness. Thus the pastor will endeavor to guide the listener along until she comes face to face with the gospel perspective of a caring God. Future discussions may be necessary to explore fully the clues found in the sermon.

These gospel assurances are often appropriate clues: God understands suffering and pain. God's Son also suffered. God is on the side of mourners. God is not their enemy. God cares for the deceased and mourners. God's love is sufficient. God is present to help. God strengthens the weak in faith. God can rebuild shattered lives now, a foretaste of life to come.

Of course technical theological language is a monumental barrier to communication. At funerals, the congregation represents various churches and beliefs. Theological vocabularies will vary. Pastors should work harder than ever to use common expressions and a conversational style.

*Hopeful images are important clues.* In the first part of the sermon images operated to mirror reality; here images function to transform reality.

In the funeral sermon the realm of hope is a unifying world made up of words/pictures and entered by words/pictures. In that world healing can take place. By transforming the awareness, the feelings, and the thoughts of mourners the sermon can bring a glimpse of the wholeness Christ promises to the broken.

It really does not matter whether images invoked are from the biblical text, the mourners' past experience, or the preacher's own world. If they *fit*, and if they capture imaginations, these pictures can be used by the Spirit to open blind eyes.

The image of a stagnant marsh was once helpful to a woman who for years had kept a summer place along the New Jersey shore. She associated marsh with lifeless water, mosquitoes, and foul odor. The image was her own; it captured her thoughts and feelings at the death of her husband. Yet that same image became a vehicle of life in the hands of a skillful pastor. The preacher described in her sermon how powered barges were used to dredge channels through tall grass, so that with each rise and fall of the tides the marshes were drained. To a woman who lived in the stagnation of depression, that image of Christ's cleansing power communicated.

It sometimes happens that an inadequate image *supplied by the mourners* must be carefully replaced. Projected in a public forum such as the funeral, an image is apt to become a focus of later pastoral conversations. A deficient image can be an impediment if allowed to stand unchallenged. For example, one pastor suggested that the image of an airplane taking off through cloud cover and breaking into cloudless blue was flawed as a picture of grief. A better analogy, the pastor suggested in his sermon, would be a plane flying through a series of cloud banks and rain squalls as it moved from stormy low pressure toward clear weather.

In a time of confusion familiar things are often most effective. Favorite Scripture passages and key themes from a pastor's normal preaching may have the best chance of breaking through barriers of shock and distraction. Trusted images (e.g., Jesus the good shepherd) will attract attention to the message and enable listeners to decode it. Images arising out of the gospel narratives of Jesus' death and resurrection exercise a power in funeral sermons that they may seem to lack in normal Sunday preaching.

Finally, the memorability of images is also significant. When a sermon ends, what remains? Major points become confused and are lost with time's passage. Feelings may linger a bit longer, but they too fade. Yet amid the chaos of grief a picture is apt to persist.

In the case we have been discussing Paul shared with the pastor his recurrent dream of waking up in a strange country beside a deserted road. He felt lost and was not sure which way to go. He felt deserted and wondered why God had abandoned him. In the second movement of the sermon the pastor is able to use that same image in a hopeful way. Jesus comes to his grieving followers on the road and goes with them on their journey. The image of being abandoned along a road was a strong picture of reality for Paul. The image of a companion on the rough journey has the promise of being equally hopeful.

Particularly if the central message of the sermon and its chief image are fused, the silhouette left in the mind has staying and pulling power. When image and content are yoked, so that the first is the kernel of the second, the image is remembered and can draw feelings and meanings back to life.

*Picture hopeful endings.* Having heard the story of the dead person and the stories of the various mourners, some resolution is needed. The preacher has the opportunity to take these stories and suggest alternative endings in light of the good news. Despair need not be the final word; hope is possible.

Guidance is important to suffering people. Their baffled state suggests that firm direction is more necessary than ever. Thus by picturing hopeful endings pastors are taking seriously a responsibility to suggest what new life can mean for believers.

This new life is pictured, not prescribed. Insofar as mourners remain sinful, dominated by the old Adam and Eve, they need an occasional touch with the lash of imperatives. Yet at the same time believing mourners respond positively to the indicative, pictures of what new life can look like. Preachers can hold out promises of what being "in Christ" can mean for mourners, while simultaneously giving them permission to live that way. Funeral preaching becomes mutual storytelling when it retells the story of death while suggesting hopeful endings that can be accepted, rejected, or altered by the listeners.

Surprisingly, resolving the story of the dead person probably requires little elaboration at this point in the sermon. Unless the individual has been an unbeliever, has committed suicide, or has died in the act of some heinous crime, the normal assumption is that the baptized person is "with Christ." Having begun with the problem of a loved one's death, ending with the gospel assurance that the individual is in God's hands gives a feeling of completion to the sermon. Even in questionable cases mourners need to hear of the amazing grace of a God who desires to save all. Further expansion may be pastorally unnecessary as well as theologically inappropriate.

Many pastors today use great restraint in speaking about the location or disposition of the dead, in part because the Scriptures themselves exercise similar caution. The dead, we are told, "sleep in Christ" or are "with the Lord." When pastors "preach the dead into heaven" by stressing only immediate glorification, they ignore the Bible's own tendency to allow statements/images suggesting immediate entrance into God's presence to stand side by side with more frequent statements/images suggesting that the dead await future translation.

Further, language stressing that the deceased is with God *now* may be a subtle denial of death. Preachers would do well to reaffirm the promise of a future with God beyond death, and leave it at that.

The congregation's story may be retold in this sermon episode with a view toward hopeful endings. An individual has died, but that death has affected (perhaps shattered) community. Personal existence is threatened when a marriage, a family, or significant friendships are ruptured. When loved ones are laid to rest a void is created that simultaneously cannot be filled and must be filled. When death threatens who we are and what we are, community must be re-created.

Who will help in this effort? Distant relatives will be going home. The attention of friends and neighbors may wane if a bereaved person's anger or depression persists. People who were part of a dead husband's constellation of associates may avoid a grieving wife. A man without a spouse may be isolated suddenly from a couples' world. Few of us have friends like Job had, who will sit day after day to hear our lament.

The church, the community of believers, has the potential to be a source of strength and support for mourners. It can provide both human relationships and a context of ultimacy where survivors can do their grief work until a vision of new life becomes plain. While human families rise and pass away, the household of faith (in a sense) transcends time and passage, giving stability and purpose. In the company of others who know alienation and suffering, and who need love and peace, mourners can reconstruct their lives. It is in the church that Christ is experienced as present. It is in the church that reconciliation overcomes alienation, and forgiveness washes away guilt.

Yet even in unity, brokenness remains. Sin persists in the lives of the redeemed, and the church is not yet what it shall be. In a community presumably full of confessors, mourners may find few willing to sit and listen or to speak a word of hope. In a community of love, some will turn their backs while others place conditions on acceptance.

While the preacher may wish to proclaim the steadfast support of the congregation, honesty may prevent it. If the community of faith has been trained to stand beside mourners while grief runs its course, the pastor should say that in the sermon. If a bereavement group exists, and if congregational members will telephone and visit mourners, shout it to the housetops. Otherwise say nothing, lest empty promises deepen frustration.

The pastor's story should be told. If the minister cannot in good conscience promise mourners a support system in the congregation, hopefully he or she can pledge pastoral care. The ministry of consolation is the task of ordained persons as much as it is the task of lay ministers. A promise to stand by sufferers and to visit can be made in the sermon, where geography and time commitments permit.

The family's story of course finally holds the other stories together. The doubts and fears of those closest to the deceased focused the section on the reality of death. A question of these mourners probably became the central concern of the sermon. Now it is time to speak directly to the family and close friends about the comfort of the gospel.

Broken lives seek repair. A preacher can support the wavering in a resolve to go on. A preacher can help dependent persons to rest in the strength God supplies. A preacher can assist mourners immobilized by fear to find hope.

We said at the outset that funeral preaching involves the sensitive juxtaposing and interweaving of three stories: the dead person's, the mourners', and God's. Now, in outline form, we are able to see one possible arrangement of these episodes in two major movements.

The Reality of Death and Loss
>    Make contact by telling the story of death.
>    Tell the mourners' stories.
>    >    The pastor's story.
>    >    The congregation's story.
>    >    The family's story.
>    Focus on one question being asked.
>    Employ an image of death or grief.

Hope: The Good News of the Gospel
>    Proclaim the good news.
>    Focus on the Christ story.
>    Employ theological clues.
>    Images of hope are important clues.
>    Picture hopeful endings.
>    >    The story of the dead person.
>    >    The congregation's story.
>    >    The pastor's story.
>    >    The family's story.

### A Sermonic Sample

When the pastor preached at Gwen's funeral this is essentially the outline that was followed. You may wish to return to pages 86–87 and see how the feelings, questions, and images introduced in movement 1 are addressed here by the good news of the gospel. In darkness come the hopeful strains of a trumpet.

In the twenty-fourth chapter of Luke's Gospel we read the story of two disciples fleeing Jerusalem. Despair was on their lips: "We had hoped that he was the one to redeem Israel."

**[When the same text speaks both to the reality of death and to the hope of new life it functions best at the heart of the sermon. Here it serves as a bridge from the first plot movement to the second.]**

Then you remember that a stranger came and walked with them. Their grief kept them from recognizing him, but the companion was

Jesus. These mourners felt forsaken, but all the while their risen Lord was at their elbows.

There is a clue in this account for us. Two mourners long ago expected their Lord to be available in hard times. They were led to believe he would stand by them. They felt alone. But the tears in their eyes prevented them from recognizing the one who came to walk with them.

[Here the word "clue" suggests that listeners construct the message of the sermon anew in their own minds and hearts.]

It is that same Jesus, risen from the dead, conqueror of the grave, who steps across the centuries to walk that lonesome road with you and me.

Paul, Jill, Jennifer, the **road** ahead is rough, full of bumps and unexpected turns. Occasionally you'll feel lost, unable to back up, afraid to take a step forward. You'll be angry when you feel neglected. You will be convinced that you have been abandoned by everyone, yes, even by God.

[The preacher is able to salvage the road image, keeping the reality of a rocky journey but sharing the good news of a companion on the way.]

But God will be there, often hidden, barely visible. Sometimes in the encouraging words of a friend, God will speak. In the passing remark of a stranger, God will be present. Surely in weekly worship the Christ who died and rose again for us will make himself known.

[The sermon is true to the text and to real life. The risen Lord is always hidden in a revelation. God speaks through other people as well as through the Scripture and meal believers experience in public worship.]

Gwen is in God's care now, and so are you, her family. While grief is a path to be walked individually (no one can "walk it for you"), it need not be walked alone. Paul, you know that many of our members will be ready to listen and care. You need not take the journey of grief by yourself.

[In respect to Gwen, the pastor reaffirms God's loving purpose. Here the pastor is able to offer the support of the members, the body of Christ.]

I do have one insight to share from the journal of believers who have traveled on before you. Grief is a bit like approaching a timbered mountain in your car. From a distance, the road seems to disappear. The barrier looks impassable. But God seldom opens paths for us in advance of our coming. The Lord rarely gives help before help is needed. Yet when obstacles rear up before us, paths become visible. As you come closer, you see the road winding up beneath the trees. Trust in God. Follow the path. God will lead you on to life, life in this world and in the world to come.

[This hopeful ending relies on both the common experience of travelers and the wisdom of those who have journeyed from grief to new life.]

## NOTES

1. Edgar Jackson, *A Psychology for Preaching* (Great Neck, N.Y.: Channel, 1961), 184.

2. John Henry Jowett, *The Preacher, His Life and Word* (New York: Doran, 1912), 133.

3. I am indebted to my friend and former colleague, Dr. Foster R. McCurley, Jr., for introducing me to this style of sentence writing as a guide for preaching. McCurley applies the method to Old Testament exegesis and proclamation in *Proclaiming the Promise* (Philadelphia: Fortress Press, 1974), 62–65.

4. H. Grady Davis, *Design for Preaching* (Philadelphia: Fortress Press, 1958), 9.

5. Ibid., 98.

6. In his classic *The Funeral and the Mourners: Pastoral Care of the Bereaved* (Nashville: Abingdon Press, 1954), Paul Irion formulates and discusses the purposes of the funeral. Many of these can be applied, in some measure, to the funeral sermon.

7. Robert Roth, *Story and Reality* (Grand Rapids: Wm. B. Eerdmans, 1973), 23–24, as quoted in Eugene Lowry, *The Homiletical Plot: The Sermon as Narrative Art Form* (Atlanta: John Knox Press, 1980), 14–15.

8. R. E. C. Browne, *The Ministry of the Word* (Philadelphia: Fortress Press, 1976), 84.

# Sermon Analysis

Preaching is an oral event. Sermons are to be heard, not read. Gestures, facial expressions, tone of voice, and body language are missing in what follows. The liturgical setting is difficult to discern from the sermon text. The relationship between pastor and people that provided a meaningful context for pastoral conversation is only partly visible. What was once a dialogical encounter between a preacher, mourners, and God cannot be reduced to words on a printed page.

The printed words, the sermon manuscripts on succeeding pages, were not prepared to be read. If they happen to read well that is purely accidental. These scripts were written word for word as one step in preparing to preach, but they were not employed as prompting devices for the auditory experience. The messages were reduced to a few words on file cards.

Of course, the names and circumstances of the persons involved have been altered to protect pastoral confidences. However, the dynamics of grief and theological questions addressed in the sermons are genuine.

It is fair to ask why these particular sermon manuscripts were chosen for analysis. Variety is the key. The ages of the deceased, the causes of death, the theological issues raised are diverse. While the sermons are models of the particular approach advocated in this book they are not carbon copies of each other. They open variously with a gripping image, with the story of the deceased, and with mourner feelings. The biblical text is employed at various locations in the message. Yet each sermon juxtaposes and interweaves God's story with that of the deceased and mourners as a way of acknowledging the reality of death while proclaiming the hope of new life in Christ.

Despite the disclaimers, a great deal can be learned by subjecting sermon manuscripts to thorough analysis. The therapist develops a counseling technique, in part, by examining verbatim material. Similarly, the analysis of sermon scripts can be a vital learning experience for the preacher. Audio and video tapes have their place in the learning process. And it is true that as the print medium focuses on the words and structure of the message it does suppress dimensions of the total event. However, this abstraction is helpful in forcing the communicator to concentrate on these essential elements. To that end, analytical comments have been included. They appear in boldface type and are set off from the sermon text by brackets.

How can these pages be used profitably? Begin by reading the brief introduction to each sermon. It places the message in context and provides clues to its interpretation. Next, ignoring the analysis read the text of the sermon *aloud* from start to finish as the best way of approximating the oral event. Only then should each scene be reread with its accompanying comments. While this procedure is painstaking, an initial sermon reading for overall impression and content with a second reading for analysis should pay rich dividends.

# I

## CONTEXT FOR PREACHING

Susan died of a massive brain infection diagnosed initially as encephalitis. Unfortunately, her parents did not permit an autopsy to be performed, so little was known about the onset and progress of the disease that resulted in her premature death.

Nancy and Mark, Susan's parents, in their middle thirties with no other children, were shocked at this senseless tragedy. In reconstructing the chain of events that led to Susan's death her distraught parents did not seem to blame themselves or the doctors. The family doctor who was called immediately recognized the potential seriousness of the fever and had Susan rushed to an excellent medical center. Unfortunately, nothing could be done. The circumstances under which this creatively brilliant eight-year-old was snatched away caused the parents to blame God.

The couple's 1967 vacation at the New Jersey seashore was the setting of the incident that opens the sermon. Nancy shared it with the pastor hours after Susan's death. For her it seemed a clue to the sinister death of her child. She readily consented to its use in the sermon. Angry feelings and questions about God's will are dealt with openly. While the cause of death is labeled, and the onus is shifted from God's shoulders, there is no assertion of easy or complete answers to tragedy. The good news of God's power over evil is related to Baptism, as Susan's death and resurrection, and to prayer for a mourning family.

The sermon was prepared to end with God's gift of peace. However, on the way to the funeral the final image hit the preacher like a bolt from the blue. Intuitions were followed and the image was used. Homiletically, it feels tacked-on. Pastorally, Nancy reported that it symbolized hope and victory.

### HOMILY

*Scripture Lesson*                                      *Mark 4:35–41*

They came to the beach early in the morning; a father, a mother, and a little girl. The sand the tide had left behind was hard and moist, perfect for building. With her plastic bucket the little girl heaped sand into a mound, packing it hard with her feet. Then she began to shape it. Her father and mother joined in. Walls were carved and a central hall appeared. Spectators gathered to watch and encourage the builders. Turrets rose into the sky, and by noon the castle was complete. The happy family surveyed its work, and went up to the boardwalk for lunch.

[The opening line captures attention. The correspondence between these three and the bereaved family is striking.]

But while the three were gone the tide returned, overflowing the moat, breaching the walls, and leveling the castle. When the family returned only a mound of sand remained where their dream castle had stood. Tears rolled down the cheeks of the little girl, and her parents felt anger and dismay.

[Contrast is one key to the impact of this funeral sermon. Building and leveling, imagination and destruction, life versus death stand against each other.]

Nancy, you told me that story, and agreed that I might use it today, because the incident captured your feelings and Mark's at the death of your little girl Susan. Susan's imagination caused flowers to appear on blank paper, created miniature villages out of modeling clay, and shaped wool into doll sweaters. The world saw level sand, but Susan shaped it into castles. Susan's dreams brought joy and excitement into your lives.

[The transition gives the story a source, a context, and a purpose. The brief examples of Susan's creative imagination support the positive image.]

And then, when you weren't looking, the tide crashed across the beach. First, a mere headache, the faintest warning. Then a high fever. A midnight ambulance ride to the hospital. Massive brain infection. Encephalitis. Susan was dead. In a matter of hours your dream castle was washed away.

[Short and incomplete sentences suggest the speed of this event.]

What sort of force is it that, like stormy waves, smashes at the foundations of our lives? What kind of world is it where, without warning, innocent life can be destroyed? What kind of God is it who could sleep through a child's death?

[The preacher gives voice to the complaint of parents and all who question needless destruction and death. The lament builds to a crescendo.]

The disciples of Jesus asked a similar question. In the fourth chapter of Mark's Gospel, we find them crossing the sea of Galilee late in the evening. Suddenly, a great storm arose. "The waves beat into the boat, so that the boat was already filling." Jesus was asleep in the stern, but the frightened disciples shouted to him, "Teacher, do you not care if we perish?"

[The transition ties the parents' angry question to that of the disciples in the biblical text. Such bridges are crucial in the oral medium.]

The story in Mark 4 does not explain the mystery of premature death. Let's be honest; there is a great deal we do not know about the power of evil in the world. The storm of death rages against those closest to Jesus, and on the cross it claimed our Lord himself. As St. Paul says, "we know in part," we see "dimly" until that day when all will be revealed.

[A theology of the cross is realistic about our lack of knowledge, but what is known about God's will and purpose can be shared. It should not come off as a defense of God.]

We do know that the world we live in is a disfigured façade of the structure that God called "good." We do know that ruthless infections and premature death were not part of God's original plan. We do know that the beautiful castle the creator erected is battered and scarred. And most of us also know the power of the storm, because at one time or another it has smashed into each of our lives.

[The castle and storm are a carrying image that gives unity and power to the sermon. Here the brief mention re-evokes the entire story. Repetition need not be redundant.]

But most important, we know, as the disciples came to know, that the Son of God has power over the forces of death and destruction. "And Jesus awoke and rebuked the wind, and said to the sea, 'Peace! Be still!' And the wind ceased, and there was a great calm."

[At this crux in the sermon the action shifts from reality to hope. The good news is Jesus' power over the forces of destruction.]

Nancy and Mark, eight years ago you brought Susan to be washed in the waters of Baptism. As a baby she rested peacefully in your arms; today Susan rests in the arms of her friend. We know that in the waters of Baptism Susan was joined to the death and resurrection of Jesus. We know that in the waters of Baptism she became a member of the church, the body of Christ. And we know that in the waters of Baptism the storm of death was stilled and life began for Susan. On the last day God will raise up Susan and all who believe to receive the gift of eternal life.

[The positive image of life-giving baptismal water is a counter to the flood of death. The refrain "we know" makes this baptismal scene a contrast to the previous "we know" section.]

Mark, Nancy, the peace Susan knows in Jesus can be yours as well. When the waves of death smashed over you, they not only took the life of your little girl, they eroded your faith as well. But you know that there are members of this congregation who have suffered losses like yours. In the months that lie ahead they will be willing to listen. I will be visiting regularly to talk and to pray with you.

[Hopeful endings are abundant. Susan is in the arms of Jesus. A church and its pastor offer support. Peace is a gospel promise.]

Sometimes death leaves us so empty it seems impossible to pray. But don't be afraid to shout to the heavens. Call to the one who sleeps in the back of the boat. He will not forsake you. The Lord who calmed the raging storm will give to you the gift of peace.

[Prayer flows out of the text and is linked to it. The sermon might have ended with peace.]

At the shore last summer I saw a sign of life and hope. Apparently in the dead of winter hundreds of dried Christmas trees were trucked to the beach. They were fastened in place where the waves had eroded the dunes, threatening property and people. During the months that followed the rising and falling tides dropped sand that was trapped and built up around the trees. In the spring the new dunes were planted with grass and life returned. This year children and their parents can come and build in safety. Castles will rise from the sand. Shouting and laughter will be heard again.

[The mourner's own image of senseless destruction on the beach cried for a hopeful ending. The pastor's story leaves a final image that may help listeners feel that the forces of evil and destruction can be overcome. The sermon is framed, both beginning and ending with laughter and hope, and feels complete.]

## II

### CONTEXT FOR PREACHING

The preacher's scanty records indicate that John was killed in an automobile accident at age fifty-five. He was a member of a local congregation of the United Church of Christ. John was buried, as Christians sometimes are, by one pastor covering for a fellow pastor who was undergoing surgery. John's biographical materials were passed on to his pastor and the burial entered in the records of the congregation.

John had never been married, and his two sisters lived on the west coast. Arrangements for burial were made over the telephone, so that the preacher met the grieving family for the first time at the viewing that preceded the funeral.

The plot line of this sermon was constructed first when it was preached at the funeral of a neighbor and friend of the preacher and his family. However, with changes it seemed to lend itself to situations where the deceased or relatives were more or less anonymous. We have said that anxiety is the emotion basic to every grief experience. The Twenty-third Psalm is loved by most Christians and frequently is known by heart. Gaps left in the plot line permitted the inclusion of comments and observations gleaned from a brief encounter with the family. Examples chosen were appropriate to a person who was apparently a sportsman and loved the out-of-doors. In this way the preacher was able to be true to both human situation and text while personalizing a message addressed to strangers. The chief image comes, as it must, from the preacher's own experience.

## HOMILY

*Scripture Lesson*                                    *Psalm 23:4*

When death reaches into our families and takes someone we love from us our thoughts are naturally disturbed, our emotions reach the breaking point, and we are filled with sorrow. When you lost John—brother, relative, friend—well-meaning persons attempted to comfort you. Some said they knew how you felt. Others told you to buck up and keep a stiff upper lip. A few suggested this death was God's will, and you shouldn't question. But somehow that peace for which you yearn is not found in the easy reassurance of human beings. Today we look instead to the word of God.

[Knowing that in the case of accidental death people tend to blame God, death is personified as the enemy. Instead of focusing on John, a person the pastor does not know, contact is made by identifying the real experiences of the mourners. Inept and uninformed comments overheard at the viewing are not critiqued, but they are gently set aside by focusing on God's word.]

These words are from Psalm 23: "Even though I walk through the valley of the shadow of death, I fear no evil; for thou art with me." In the Israel the writer of this familiar poem knew so well, a land that was largely dry and rocky, there wasn't a great deal of good pasture land to be found. When the best grass in a place had been consumed it became necessary to move a flock of sheep from one meadow to another. Of course the shepherd selected the safest route, but occasionally narrow valleys could not be avoided. In these shadowy places death lurked in the form of wild animals who waited to pounce upon timid sheep.

[The shepherd image of Psalm 23 and John 10 is at once powerful and reassuring. The visual focus of Jesus as good shepherd is familiar to almost every Christian. Thus there is great likelihood that it will communicate. Again, the shepherd leads the safest way, but death waits to pounce. The shepherd is not to blame. The real cause of death will be labeled. It was an accident.]

And so it is in life. Jesus, the good shepherd, seeks always to guide us along safe paths. But there are places in life's journey that hold real danger for us in the form of trouble, illness, and accident. Sometimes these result in death, as they did for John.

Death usually has the quality of surprise, both for the person who dies and for loved ones. We are never fully ready. We are never quite prepared. Because death leaps upon us unaware, fear is a feeling most experience.

[Anxiety (fear) is the basic emotion of grief. Therefore this sermon will hit the mark in virtually every case.]

There will be those who seek to deny death and its power. The hunter or fisherman walking along a lonely mountain path sees moving shadows behind every tree and bush. But things that cause the heart to skip a beat at dusk tend to vanish in the searching light of day. Shadows aren't real . . . but death is.

[A repertoire of examples is necessary to personalize this section. At the viewing the pastor discovered that John was an outdoor person and chose this scene.]

And yet . . . Jesus passed through the valley of death before us. He walked the path to Golgotha. One day you and I must walk that way. But because our Lord conquered death, the path will not dead-end. As the poet said, "Death is a path that must be trod, if man would ever pass to God."

[Passage through the valley traversed first by the shepherd becomes a unifying image that moves the mourner from the experience of death to the hope of new life.]

Even in this journey we have a companion. The psalmist wrote, "Even though I walk through the valley of the shadow of death, I fear no evil; for thou art with me." When we walk in the sunshine and life is good we often take God's companionship for granted. In the shadows our own grief may mask God's presence. But the psalmist was able to affirm, "I fear no evil; for thou art with me."

[Christ as companion is a clue for mourners who may feel alone.]

How is God with us? How is the comforting presence of the Good Shepherd experienced? In worship we hear God's Word read and preached. God prepares a table for us some call Holy Communion, Mass, or the Lord's Supper. The Good Shepherd also comes to us through the presence of friends and relatives who gather round in the darkness.

[Yet it is necessary to address the question of how Christ is present. The terms for the Eucharist are those native to the denominations represented.]

When my grandmother was dying our family would go in the evenings to sit with her. As the pain worsened she would say, "I hear the children singing." It didn't make any sense to me, but eventually my father figured it out. As a little girl in her native Wales my grandmother, the youngest in the family, would be sent to bed first. Up in the shadowed loft, as she huddled alone and afraid, the rest of the family gathered around the piano. The sound of voices raised in Welsh hymns calmed her trembling heart. "I hear the children singing." Seventy years later, in the darkness of death, her fears were eased and the memory of her family became a channel for the comforting presence of God. "Even though I walk through the valley of the shadow of death, I fear no evil: for thou art with me."

[When there is little or no opportunity for dialogue with the mourners and the discovery of helpful texts, clues, and images from their experiences, pastors may use material from their own experience. The story is readily understandable and, especially for older persons, it is effective. Anyone who has ever been afraid in the dark can relate to that life experience.]

### III

### CONTEXT FOR PREACHING

George Williams died at the age of seventy-one after a five-year struggle with cancer. George's leukemia was attacked using an early form of chemotherapy administered in the local doctor's office. That treatment probably prolonged his life a number of years.

In his own circle of friends George was a hometown hero. Not only did his job involve the protection of fellow miners from needless risk, but his refusal to alter safety reports and his subsequent firing were local mythology. His death became an opportunity to celebrate what George represented to colleagues, friends, community, and congregation.

The preacher approaches the bounds of eulogy in relating at length the story of George's courage. George is held up as an example to the saints, but the portrait is of a real human being who knew both fear and courage. More important, in George's own testimony God receives the glory.

There is some risk that listeners will take the image of descent into the earth literally and make of George the wrong kind of Christ figure. In the sense that he lived a life of service to others without thought for his own well-being George did model what taking up one's cross can mean in a particular situation. But in the end it is clearly our Lord Christ who overcomes death and gives courage to the fearful.

## HOMILY

*Scripture Lesson*                                        *Matt. 28:1–10*

When I think of George Williams the word that hits me first is "courage." Until five years ago George was a robust former coal miner enjoying his retirement. Then leukemia began devouring the red blood cells and bone marrow that supply energy and life. At first only his family, Margaret and Beth, knew the struggle that George was mounting. In those years he never missed a church council meeting. George was a regular usher, and in time we all began to notice his failing. Three Sundays ago, when he received the offering for the last time, George barely could support the plate. By Thursday our friend was dead, and the whole family here at St. John's will miss him.

[The repetition of the word courage sets the theme for the sermon. The story of George's faithful involvement in the life of the congregation during his bout with cancer is testimony to that courage. The mental image of George's decline from one hundred and ninety pounds to one hundred and ten pounds at his death is vivid in the minds of those with whom he lived and worshiped.]

Courage! George grew up in these narrow valleys where young men often went into the mines before they were fully grown. At thirteen he was picking slate in a breaker, separating rock from coal with his bare hands. A contract miner most of his working years, George became a "fire boss" in his fifties. That job involved entering the dark tunnels before the first shift of the day to check the workings for weakened timbers, rock slides, and especially deadly gas. Forty years ago George's predecessor would have carried a canary in a cage, holding the bird ahead of him close to the floor, hoping that the deadly "coal damp" would kill the bird as a warning. With his own special lamp George stalked that underground world to make the way safe for hundreds of miners who would follow.

[A person's employment is frequently a resource for telling the story of death. George's daily descent into the tunnels of a deep, anthracite coal mine to ensure the safety of fellow miners was seen by the preacher as a striking parallel to Jesus' own descent into the hell of death for the salvation of all.]

Courage! Nine years ago there was an especially cold winter. Production was down and coal was in short supply. One February morning a company official asked George to certify that the tunnels were safe. George refused, because he had detected gas that morning. He was told the penalty for refusal, but again he said no. George was fired.

I talked to George about courage just a week ago in the hospital. The black lung had reduced his capacity for oxygen. I saw our friend's haggard face through the distorted plastic of an oxygen tent. I knew his story. I had witnessed the struggle of the past five years. But George seemed calm. "How do you do it," I stumbled, "how do you stay so . . . strong?" He managed a faint smile. George was a man of few words, and I didn't necessarily expect an answer. But he struggled to respond. "Right now I'm scared to death, but I just put my life in the Lord's hands. I'm not alone!"

[Just at the point where George's own story comes close to being a eulogy (overpraise), and where George becomes a kind of Christ figure, the source of his strength is clarified. The good news is that courage for both the dying and bereaved can be a gift of God, and that even when courage fails God does not. The quote from pastoral conversation with George is the crux where this sermon shifts from reality to hope.]

George's Lord knew both fear and courage. In Gethsemane Jesus prayed, "If you will, let this cup pass from me." He sweated drops of blood in the struggle with his emotions and his mission. But, strengthened by his Father's presence, Jesus rose from prayer to face the torches and spears of the soldiers, as well as the nails of the cross. When his own courage faltered, Jesus put his life in God's hands and was strengthened.

[The earthly Jesus experienced fear. That reminder is reassuring to the faint-hearted. The cross and (later) the resurrection of Jesus reinforce the good news by providing a basis for it.]

Margaret, Beth, I sense the turmoil you must be feeling. Suddenly life is uncertain. That pillar of strength, a husband and father, is dead. You must tremble at the thought of being alone. But you are not alone. Together, all of us are part of the church, the body of Christ. Each day, whether you brim with courage or quake with fear, we are here to support you, and the one who overcame death stands beside you.

[Dependent persons who rely on one family member for strength experience his or her death as especially traumatic. In the church, the body of Christ, the risen Lord is present. God alone can fill the void.]

On Good Friday Jesus entered the dark tunnels of death. He stalked that underground world to engage the forces of darkness and destruction. And on Easter Day he showed himself alive to Mary Magdalene and the other Mary. The guards trembled, but Jesus said to the women, "Do not be afraid; go and tell" my disciples. Jesus was victorious over death, and he is alive today. Even in the midst of grief he makes the way safe for all of us who struggle to follow.

[The Easter story provides a parallel image to George's daily journey, but with a qualitative difference. Jesus conquers, not just daily fear, but death itself.]

Margaret, Beth, the days and months ahead will not be easy. You will find yourself asking, "How can I go on without George?" But there is one source of strength. George said it: "I'm scared to death, but I just put my life in the Lord's hands. I'm not alone!"

[This is a realistic but hopeful ending. The repetition of the quote provides a frame and a sense of closure.]